Sunset
Quick Cuisine

By the Editors of Sunset Books and Sunset Magazine

Sunset Publishing Corporation ▪ Menlo Park, California

Research & Text
Cynthia Scheer

Contributing Editor
Susan Warton

Coordinating Editor
Linda J. Selden

Design
Joe di Chiarro

Illustrations
Susan Jaekel

Photography
Nikolay Zurek

Photo Stylist
JoAnn Masaoka

Cover: Veal with Olives & Dried Tomatoes (recipe on page 92), accompanied by fresh spinach fettuccine, is an elegant, Italian-style meal that takes just 35 minutes to prepare. Design by Sandra Popovich. Photography by Nikolay Zurek. Photo styling by JoAnn Masaoka. Food styling by Cynthia Scheer.

Editor, Sunset Books: Elizabeth L. Hogan

Fourth printing December 1991

Dinner's Ready!

In today's hurry-up world, many of us have little time to spend in the kitchen cooking dinner. But, in spite of our changing habits, our standards of food quality, freshness, flavor, and overall enjoyment have never been higher. Only at home in the kitchen can such quality be assured regularly—which is why we created this cook book. Look through our guide to shortcuts on page 4, study the photographs throughout the book, and, above all, sample our tempting recipes. You'll soon learn that it takes only a few minutes and a few superb ingredients to create great meals, even on the busiest nights of the week.

For our recipes, we provide a nutritional analysis prepared by Hill Nutrition Associates, Inc., of New York, stating calorie count; grams of protein, carbohydrates, and total fat; and milligrams of cholesterol and sodium. Generally, the nutritional information applies to a single serving, based on the largest number of servings given for each recipe.

The nutritional analysis does not include optional ingredients or those for which no specific amount is stated. If an ingredient is listed with an option, the information was calculated using the first choice. Likewise, if a range is given for the amount of an ingredient, values were figured based on the first, lower amount.

For their generosity in sharing props for use in our photographs, we thank The Best of All Worlds, Crate & Barrel, Menlo Park Hardware, and Williams-Sonoma. Our special thanks go to Fran Feldman for carefully editing the manuscript.

All of the recipes in this book were tested and developed in the *Sunset* test kitchens.

Sunset Magazine's test kitchens are under the supervision of Jerry Anne Di Vecchio, Home Economics Editor, *Sunset* Magazine.

Contents

Baked Cornish Hens with Vegetables (recipe on page 72) offers a sumptuous entrée, surrounded here by the carrots, potatoes, and shallots that shared its pan, as well as steamed whole green beans. Complete this hearty repast with hot dinner rolls and a chilled white wine.

Shortcuts to Good Cooking

It's one of life's ironies that, as intriguing new foods become more abundantly available, the time we have for enjoying them seems to shrink to mere minutes. Now that we truly appreciate the art of fine cuisine, we're simply too busy to savor it very often.

For most good cooks today, the answer to this time pressure is to make the most of every minute spent in the kitchen. To create great meals briefly can be a challenge at first, but it's a culinary skill that can be mastered.

Less is often more

Many of the most stylish entrées in fine restaurants are grilled, stir-fried, broiled, or quickly sautéed—cooking methods that take a minimum of time. Vegetables served alongside are almost invariably briefly steamed.

Many of us who appreciate good food have recently learned that, in cooking, the less time some foods are cooked, the more flavorful they are. Fish is moister and more succulent if cooked until barely opaque at the center. Delicate vegetables keep their color, flavor, and natural crispness if cooked just until tender.

Organizing for efficiency

Besides their quick cooking methods, good restaurants follow another principle that can help you speed up meal preparation at home. If you've ever visited a restaurant kitchen, you may have wondered how so many dishes could emerge so quickly from its often cramped physical space. The secret is organization.

Most tasks in cooking involve three work centers—the refrigerator area, the range area, and the vicinity of the sink. You can make those areas more efficient if you store the utensils appropriate to each one near where they'll be used. For example, you'll want to keep plastic bags and storage containers handy to the refrigerator. Make sure that spoons, spatulas, pans, and pot holders are easily reached from the range. Locate a chopping block, colander, knives, and cleanup materials near the sink.

Planning your strategy

A few minutes taken to organize your menus and understand your recipes can save time and frustration.

Planning menus on a day-to-day basis is inefficient; it forces you to spend extra time thinking about what to cook, and extra time in the supermarket. Instead, plot out a week's worth of menus at a time and, whenever possible, do your shopping all at once. When planning menus and when cooking, always keep simplicity in mind, but consider as well the flavor, texture, appearance, and nutritional content of the food. Remember the following tips; they'll help when you sit down to plan menus that are simple and quick to prepare, yet interesting to eat.

- Provide a good variety of color, flavor, shape, temperature, and texture in the foods you arrange together in a menu.

- When you're planning to cook two or three dishes at once, use different cooking techniques. You wouldn't want to serve sautéed fish with stir-fried vegetables; there would be too much simultaneous activity on the range, all just before serving time. Instead, pair the stir-fried vegetables with baked fish.

- Plan ahead for leftovers. If you have time to roast chicken on Sunday, roast two; then, on Tuesday night, you might use the leftover chicken in a quick main-dish salad.

- Prepare ingredients ahead of time, whenever possible, to save valuable minutes during meal preparation. Shred cheese and keep it refrigerated in glass jars. Wash, dry, and store salad greens as soon as you bring them home from the market.

- Schedule your meals for smooth serving, with everything ready at once. Base your schedule on the time you'll serve the meal, and then work backward from serving time, creating a workable plan.

Time-saving tools

Using well-designed utensils correctly and appropriately increases your efficiency in the kitchen. Sharp knives are a must for today's fresh, light, and quick cuisine. Store them in a protected place, such as a wooden block or magnetic rack. Hone your own chopping and slicing skills so you can use knives to the greatest advantage—and save time.

Your food processor is also a great time-saver. Let it speed up the chopping, slicing, and shredding of vegetables, cheeses, and other foods. Often, it isn't necessary to wash the processor between preparing several ingredients for the same dish; just start with the one that makes the least mess.

When time is short, the microwave oven can be another boon to the busy cook. Many of the recipes in this book offer microwave instructions; in addition, you can use your microwave in innumerable other ways, such as to melt or soften butter, to soften cream cheese or frozen juice concentrate, to warm bread or tortillas, or to thaw frozen meats or poultry.

Another invaluable tool that you may have overlooked are someone's helping hands, especially welcome when you're in a hurry. Enlist anyone you can— even if it's just to set the table, get out serving dishes, slice bread, light candles, or open a bottle of wine.

Food on hand

Always keep a well-stocked larder and replenish your supplies before they run out. These basic foods should always be in stock: sugar, flour, and salt in your pantry; spices and herbs conveniently arranged in a cool place away from direct light; and eggs, dairy products, mayonnaise, and mustard in the refrigerator.

Other handy ingredients include versatile hard-cooked eggs; butter that's been flavored with herbs, garlic, or grated lemon or orange peel to season vegetables or broiled fish, poultry, or meats; toasted nuts to include in salads or desserts; and buttered, seasoned bread crumbs to top casseroles or baked tomato halves.

Though our recipes generally specify fresh ingredients wherever time permits, we frequently rely on canned tomato sauce and tomatoes, as well as chicken and beef broth. A tube of tomato paste in the refrigerator is useful for squeezing out a teaspoon or tablespoon at a time to enrich a sauce.

Shopping tips

If you have too little time to cook, chances are that you have even less time to shop. Yet, for many of us, a quick stop at the supermarket after work has become part of life's hectic routine. However, making just one thorough shopping trip each week can actually save precious time, energy, and money, and may even result in less wasted food.

Approach shopping as an adventure. Choose a conveniently located store that has high standards of quality, a broad selection of fresh and packaged foods, and a polite and helpful staff. Map out the store's floor plan; then structure your shopping list according to its departments.

Many products on the market today offer such healthful options as low-sodium or low-fat content; other foods may be all natural, or sugar- or caffeine-free. Read labels and become savvy about what you're buying, cooking with, and consuming.

Also, be fussy about freshness. Besides looking and tasting better, fresh foods also offer top nutrition.

For even easier menus, shop in a supermarket that has a good deli. Many such stores sell easy-to-cook or no-cook items, from assorted salads to succulent roast chickens.

Full-meal Soups

*Like a garden-fresh minestrone, Chicken &
Capellini Soup (recipe on facing page) presents swirls of
pasta with colorful vegetables. Each ingredient goes into the pot at just the
right moment to keep its color and flavor intact.*

Contrary to popular belief, good soup doesn't have to involve hours of stirring, skimming, and simmering. Many marvelous soups come together in well under an hour. It's simply a matter of selecting ingredients that will contribute full, rich flavor after only minutes in the soup pot, ingredients such as boneless chicken and turkey, savory sausage, and fresh fish and shellfish. Add convenient canned broth—or homemade from the freezer, if you prefer—and fresh vegetables for accent, and you can produce satisfying soup from scratch any night of the week.

Autumn Vegetable & Turkey Chowder

PREPARATION TIME COOKING TIME
MINUTES   MINUTES

When you have leftover roast turkey, this colorful and creamy soup, enriched with golden Cheddar cheese, serves up a delectable encore. Bake a pan of cornbread to serve alongside.

   3   tablespoons butter or margarine
   1   medium-size onion, chopped
   1   cup thinly sliced carrots
   ½   cup thinly sliced celery
   2   cups diced potatoes
   1   can (about 1 lb.) tomatoes
   2   beef bouillon cubes
   1½ teaspoons Worcestershire
   2   cups diced cooked turkey
   2   cups milk
       Salt and pepper
   1½ cups (6 oz.) shredded sharp Cheddar cheese
       Chopped parsley

In a 3-quart pan, melt butter over medium heat. Add onion and cook until limp (3 to 5 minutes). Stir in carrots, celery, potatoes, tomatoes (break up with a spoon) and their liquid, bouillon cubes, and Worcestershire. Increase heat to high and bring to a boil; reduce heat, cover, and boil gently, stirring occasionally, until vegetables are tender (20 to 25 minutes). Mix in turkey.

Gradually stir in milk; heat, stirring often, just until soup is steaming. Season with salt and pepper to taste; then add 1¼ cups of the cheese, stirring until cheese is melted. Ladle soup into bowls; sprinkle with parsley and remaining ¼ cup cheese. Makes 4 to 6 servings.

Per serving: 367 calories, 26 g protein, 21 g carbohydrates, 20 g total fat, 93 mg cholesterol, 725 mg sodium

Chicken & Capellini Soup

(Pictured on facing page)

PREPARATION TIME COOKING TIME
MINUTES   MINUTES

Tender strands of capellini swirl through this substantial chicken and vegetable soup. Enjoy the quick and appetizing meal-in-a-bowl with a loaf of crusty Italian bread, a selection of cheeses, and fresh fruit.

   2   whole chicken breasts (about 1 lb. *each*), skinned, boned, and split
   2   tablespoons butter or margarine
   ¼   cup finely chopped shallots
   1   clove garlic, minced or pressed
   ½   teaspoon salt
   ¼   teaspoon dry thyme
   ⅛   teaspoon white pepper
   1   can (14½ oz.) regular-strength chicken broth
   1½ cups water
   ½   cup dry white wine
   1   medium-size carrot, thinly sliced
   2   ounces dry capellini (angel-hair pasta), broken in half
   2   cups shredded Swiss chard leaves
   1   medium-size tomato, seeded and chopped
       Grated Parmesan cheese

Cut chicken into bite-size pieces; set aside.

In a deep 3½- to 4-quart pan, melt butter over medium heat. Add shallots and cook, stirring often, until soft but not browned (2 to 3 minutes). Stir in garlic, salt, thyme, white pepper, and chicken. Cook, stirring often, until chicken is white and opaque-looking (about 3 minutes). Add broth, water, wine, and carrot. Bring to a boil over high heat; reduce heat, cover, and boil gently until carrot is tender (about 15 minutes).

Add capellini. Bring again to a boil over high heat and cook, uncovered, stirring often, until pasta is *al dente* (4 to 5 minutes). Add chard and tomato; cover, remove from heat, and let stand just until tomato is heated through (about 2 minutes). Offer cheese to add to individual portions. Makes 4 servings.

Per serving: 328 calories, 42 g protein, 18 g carbohydrates, 8 g total fat, 112 mg cholesterol, 945 mg sodium

Chinese Chicken & Shrimp Soup

PREPARATION TIME MINUTES   MINUTES COOKING TIME

This light Asian-style soup is ready almost as soon as it boils. Once you've prepared its nourishing ingredients—chicken, shrimp, tofu, and vegetables—there's little left to do but savor the result.

1   whole chicken breast (about 1 lb.), skinned, boned, and split
1¼ quarts regular-strength chicken broth
2   tablespoons finely chopped fresh ginger
2   to 3 teaspoons soy sauce
6   ounces mushrooms, sliced (about 2½ cups)
3   cups thinly sliced bok choy
1   cup firm tofu cubes (about ½ inch square)
½   cup sliced green onions (including tops)
½   pound small cooked shrimp
¼   cup chopped fresh cilantro (coriander)
    Ground red pepper (cayenne) or chili oil (optional)

Cut chicken into ½-inch cubes; set aside.

Pour broth into a 4- to 5-quart pan; add ginger and soy sauce. Bring to a boil over high heat. Add chicken, mushrooms, bok choy, tofu, and onions. Cook, uncovered, until chicken is no longer pink in center when cut (about 2 minutes). Remove pan from heat and stir in shrimp and cilantro. Season with red pepper to taste, if desired. Makes 4 to 6 servings.

Per serving: 170 calories, 28 g protein, 4 g carbohydrates, 3 g total fat, 89 mg cholesterol, 1125 mg sodium

Rich & Spicy Potato-Shrimp Soup

PREPARATION TIME MINUTES   MINUTES COOKING TIME

A confetti of crumbled bacon and diced bell pepper brightens this potato soup, dotted with tiny shrimp and seasoned with jalapeño chiles. Honor the Mexican influence by passing around warm, buttered tortillas.

6   slices bacon
6   fresh jalapeño chiles, seeded and finely chopped
1   medium-size onion, finely chopped
1   cup diced celery
½   cup seeded, diced red bell pepper
4   cloves garlic, minced or pressed
1½ cups water
6   medium-size thin-skinned potatoes (about 2 lbs.), peeled and diced
2   cups whipping cream
3   cups milk
¼   cup dry white wine
1   cup (about ½ lb.) small cooked shrimp
    Salt and pepper

In a wide frying pan, cook bacon over medium heat until crisp. Lift out, drain, and crumble; set aside. Discard all but 2 tablespoons of the drippings.

Add chiles, onion, celery, bell pepper, and garlic to pan. Cook, stirring occasionally, until vegetables are tender-crisp (6 to 8 minutes).

Meanwhile, in a 4- to 5-quart pan, bring water to a boil over high heat. Add potatoes; reduce heat, cover, and boil gently until tender (10 to 12 minutes). Stir in cooked vegetables, cream, milk, wine, and shrimp; season with salt and pepper to taste. Cover and cook over low heat until steaming (about 3 minutes). Pour into a soup tureen and garnish with bacon. Makes 4 or 5 servings.

Per serving: 684 calories, 26 g protein, 52 g carbohydrates, 43 g total fat, 205 mg cholesterol, 352 mg sodium

Yaquina Bay Salmon Chowder

PREPARATION TIME MINUTES   MINUTES COOKING TIME

From Oregon's seacoast comes this chowder of exceptional elegance. The rich, delicate broth, enhanced by a sprinkling of Cheddar cheese, makes a dignified setting for succulent salmon.

1   can (10¾ oz.) condensed chicken broth
1   bottle (8 oz.) clam broth
1   cup dry white wine
2   pounds salmon steaks or fillets (about 1 inch thick)
6   tablespoons butter or margarine
1   medium-size onion, chopped
2   stalks celery, chopped
¼   teaspoon *each* dry basil, thyme, and marjoram
1½ cups milk
1   can (1 lb. 12 oz.) tomatoes, drained and chopped
1   tablespoon brandy

Salt and pepper
About 1½ cups (6 oz.) shredded Cheddar cheese

In a wide frying pan, combine chicken broth, clam broth, and wine. Bring to a boil over high heat; reduce heat and place salmon in liquid. Cover and simmer until salmon is opaque at bone or in center when cut (10 to 12 minutes). Lift out salmon and let cool slightly; then remove and discard bones, skin, and any gray brown edges. Flake salmon and set aside; reserve poaching liquid.

Meanwhile, in a 4- to 5-quart pan, melt butter over medium heat. Add onion and celery and cook, stirring often, until onion is soft (about 5 minutes). Stir in basil, thyme, marjoram, milk, tomatoes, and poaching liquid. Cover and cook gently for 10 minutes. Add salmon, stir in brandy, and season with salt and pepper to taste. Ladle into bowls. Offer cheese to add to individual portions. Makes 4 to 6 servings.

Per serving: 611 calories, 44 g protein, 13 g carbohydrates, 42 g total fat, 125 mg cholesterol, 1129 mg sodium

Riviera Fish Soup

PREPARATION TIME   COOKING TIME

Fragrant with garlic and herbs, this tomato-based soup is both hearty and easy. If you prefer, you can cook it right in a soup tureen in your microwave oven—or, in traditional fashion, on top of the range.

> 1 **tablespoon olive oil or salad oil**
> 1 **small onion, sliced**
> 1 **clove garlic, minced or pressed**
> ¼ **cup sliced celery**
> 2 **tablespoons chopped parsley**
> ½ **teaspoon Italian herb seasoning or ⅛ teaspoon *each* dry basil, oregano, thyme, and marjoram**
>   **Dash of ground red pepper (cayenne)**
> 1 **can (10¾ oz.) condensed tomato soup**
> 2 **tablespoons tomato paste**
> 1¼ **cups hot water**
> 1 **can (6½ or 8 oz.) chopped or minced clams**
> ¼ **pound small cooked shrimp**
> 1 **pound Greenland turbot or rockfish fillets, cut into 1½-inch squares**
>   **Salt and black pepper**

Heat oil in a 3-quart pan over medium heat. Stir in onion, garlic, and celery and cook until onion is limp (about 4 minutes). Stir in parsley, Italian herb seasoning, red pepper, tomato soup, tomato paste, water,

clams and their liquid, shrimp, and fish. Bring to a boil; reduce heat, cover, and simmer until fish flakes easily when prodded with a fork (about 15 minutes). Season with salt and black pepper to taste. Ladle into wide soup plates or deep bowls. Makes 3 or 4 servings.

Per serving: 250 calories, 33 g protein, 14 g carbohydrates, 7 g total fat, 120 mg cholesterol, 772 mg sodium

To Microwave: In a 2½- to 3-quart microwave-safe casserole or soup tureen, mix oil, onion, garlic, and celery. Microwave, covered, on **HIGH (100%)** for 8 minutes, stirring 2 or 3 times, until onion is limp. Add parsley, Italian herb seasoning, red pepper, tomato soup, and tomato paste. Stir in water, clams and their liquid, shrimp, and fish. Microwave, covered, on **HIGH (100%)** for 8 to 10 minutes, stirring 2 or 3 times, until liquid is steaming hot and fish flakes easily when prodded in thickest part with a fork. Season and serve as directed.

Stocking up on Chicken Broth

Canned broth, though convenient, tends to be salty. If you're watching your sodium intake, you may prefer to make salt-free chicken stock.

Homemade Chicken Broth. Rinse 5 pounds **bony chicken pieces** (wings, backs, necks, carcasses) and place in a 6- to 8-quart pan. Add 2 large **onions,** cut into chunks; 2 large **carrots,** cut into chunks; 6 to 8 **parsley sprigs;** ½ teaspoon **whole black peppercorns;** and 3½ quarts **water.** Bring to a boil over high heat; reduce heat, cover, and simmer for 3 hours. Let cool.

Pour broth through a fine strainer into a bowl; discard scraps. Cover broth and refrigerate for at least 4 hours or for up to 2 days. Lift off and discard fat. To store, freeze in 1-cup to 1-quart portions. Makes about 10 cups.

Steamed Clams with Linguisa & Pasta

(Pictured on facing page)

PREPARATION TIME   COOKING TIME

Spicy linguisa sausage joins clams steamed in a richly flavored broth, dotted with tiny pasta and diced red bell pepper. For steaming, choose littleneck or Manila clams from the Pacific, littlenecks or cherrystones from the Atlantic.

> 2 **tablespoons salad oil**
> ⅓ **pound linguisa sausage, sliced ¼ inch thick**
> 1 **medium-size onion, chopped**
> 1 **large red bell pepper, seeded and diced**
> 3 **cups water**
> 1½ **cups regular-strength chicken broth**
> ¾ **cup dry white wine**
> ¼ **cup rice-shaped or other tiny pasta**
> ½ **teaspoon dry basil**
> 32 **to 36 clams suitable for steaming, well scrubbed**
> **Minced parsley**

In a 5- to 6-quart pan, combine oil and sausage; cook over medium-high heat, stirring, until sausage is lightly browned. Add onion and bell pepper; cook, stirring, until onion is limp (2 to 3 minutes). Add water, broth, wine, pasta, and basil. Cover and simmer until pasta is *al dente* (8 to 10 minutes).

Skim off and discard fat. Add clams. Cover and bring to a boil; reduce heat and simmer until clams open (5 to 7 minutes).

Lift out clams and distribute equally in 4 wide, shallow bowls. Ladle broth over clams. Lightly sprinkle each serving with parsley. Makes 4 servings.

Per serving: 388 calories, 33 g protein, 28 g carbohydrates, 14 g total fat, 142 mg cholesterol, 1120 mg sodium

Steamed Mussels with Linguisa, Leeks & Rice

Follow directions for Steamed Clams with Linguisa & Pasta, but omit onion, red bell pepper, rice-shaped pasta, basil, and clams. Slice 2 or 3 **leeks,** using only white and pale green parts.

To browned linguisa add leeks and 1 clove **garlic,** minced or pressed. Cook, stirring, until leeks are limp. Add ¼ cup **long-grain white rice** and ½ teaspoon

dry thyme with water, broth, and wine. Cover and simmer until rice is almost tender (12 to 15 minutes).

Meanwhile, scrub 3 pounds **mussels;** pull out or cut off tough brown hairlike "beard." Add mussels to skimmed broth mixture; simmer and serve as directed.

Italian Tomato & Basil Soup

PREPARATION TIME   COOKING TIME

Hot or cold, this soup is as easy as a summer breeze, and as delicious. For a light meal, serve it with chunks of savory focaccia and a wedge of your favorite sharp cheese.

> 2 **tablespoons olive oil or salad oil**
> 2 **pounds pear-shaped tomatoes, coarsely chopped**
> ½ **cup lightly packed fresh basil leaves**
> ½ **cup *each* regular-strength chicken broth and whipping cream**
> **Salt and pepper**

Heat oil in a 3- to 4-quart pan over medium-high heat. Add tomatoes and ¼ cup of the basil. Cook, stirring often, until tomatoes mash easily (10 to 15 minutes). Transfer mixture to a blender or food processor; add broth and cream. Whirl until smoothly puréed. Season with salt and pepper to taste.

Reheat to serve hot; or, to serve cold, let cool, then cover and refrigerate until thoroughly chilled or for up to a day. Sliver remaining ¼ cup basil and sprinkle over individual portions. Makes 4 servings.

Per serving: 199 calories, 3 g protein, 12 g carbohydrates, 17 g total fat, 33 mg cholesterol, 155 mg sodium

To Microwave: Combine oil, tomatoes, and the ¼ cup basil in a 3- to 4-quart microwave-safe casserole. Microwave, covered, on **HIGH (100%)** for 10 to 12 minutes, stirring 2 or 3 times, until tomatoes mash easily.

Purée tomato mixture with broth and cream and season as directed. Microwave to reheat, if desired, and serve as directed.

*Pluck steamed clams from their shells to savor
with spicy linguisa and tiny rice-shaped pasta in a steaming,
basil-flecked broth. Break off chunks of crusty sourdough bread to soak up the
broth from Steamed Clams with Linguisa & Pasta (recipe on facing page).*

Easy Appetizers

Nibbling something to whet the appetite while waiting for dinner is a popular and time-honored custom. Even when time is short, there are plenty of quick and easy possibilities. Much more imaginative than packaged products, the appetizers and first courses below are almost as effortless to prepare and serve. As for taste, they're irresistible!

Broiled Avocado Salad

   Caesar Dressing (recipe follows)
 3 medium-size ripe avocados
 4 teaspoons grated Parmesan cheese
 ½ pound small cooked shrimp
 ¼ cup shredded jack cheese
   Salt

Prepare Caesar Dressing; set aside.

   Cut avocados in half lengthwise; remove and discard pits. With a small sharp knife, score avocado just to shells (not through them), cutting into ½-inch squares.

   Mix Parmesan cheese, shrimp, and dressing; mound mixture into cavities of avocados. Arrange avocados in an 8- or 9 inch square pan. Sprinkle filling with jack cheese.

   Broil about 4 inches from heat until jack cheese is melted and avocados are partially warmed (5 to 6 minutes). Season with salt to taste and serve hot. Makes 6 first-course servings.

Caesar Dressing. Combine ¼ cup **salad oil**, 3 tablespoons **red wine vinegar**, 1 tablespoon **lemon juice**, 2 teaspoons **Dijon mustard**, 1 teaspoon **anchovy paste** or

drained, minced canned anchovies, and ¼ teaspoon **pepper**; mix well.

Per serving: 314 calories, 13 g protein, 8 g carbohydrates, 27 g total fat, 62 mg cholesterol, 167 mg sodium

Lime- & Chili-spiked Vegetables

 24 radishes, roots trimmed
 1 pound jicama, peeled
 3 tablespoons *each* lime juice and tequila (or all lime juice)
 2 tablespoons chili powder
 1 teaspoon salt

Remove all but a few leaves from each radish. Cut jicama lengthwise into ½-inch-wide, ½-inch-thick sticks. Arrange vegetables in a dish or basket. (At this point, you may cover and refrigerate for up to a day.)

   In a small bowl, mix lime juice and tequila. In another bowl, mix chili powder and salt. To eat, dip vegetables into lime mixture, then into chili mixture. Makes 8 to 10 appetizer servings.

Per serving: 34 calories, .83 g protein, 5 g carbohydrates, .39 g total fat, 0 mg cholesterol, 241 mg sodium

Pita Crisps

 6 pocket breads (6 inches in diameter)
 ¼ cup olive oil
 1 clove garlic, minced or pressed
   Freshly ground pepper

Split pocket breads apart to make 12 rounds. Mix oil and garlic. Brush split sides of bread with oil mixture and sprinkle with pepper. Cut each round into quarters. Arrange in a single layer on 2 baking sheets. Bake in a 400° oven until crisp and golden (5 to 10 minutes). Serve warm or at room temperature. Makes 4 dozen appetizers.

Per crisp: 32 calories, .67 g protein, 5 g carbohydrates, 1 g total fat, 0 mg cholesterol, 45 mg sodium

Asparagus Spears with Watercress Mayonnaise

 1 egg
 1 tablespoon white wine vinegar
 1 teaspoon *each* Dijon mustard and anchovy paste
 ⅓ cup packed watercress leaves
 1 small clove garlic (optional)
 1 cup salad oil
 24 to 36 asparagus spears

In a blender or food processor, combine egg, vinegar, mustard, anchovy paste, watercress, and, if desired, garlic. Whirl until smooth. With motor running, add oil in a thin, steady stream until smoothly absorbed. (At this point, you may cover and refrigerate mayonnaise for up to 2 days.)

   Snap off and discard tough ends of asparagus. Bring 1 inch of water to a boil in a wide frying pan. Add asparagus and boil, uncovered, until barely tender (3 to 4 minutes). Drain, immerse in cold water, and drain again. Serve asparagus at room temperature or chilled to dip into mayonnaise. Makes 10 to 12 appetizer servings.

Per serving of asparagus: 10 calories, 1 g protein, 2 g carbohydrates, .09 g total fat, 0 mg cholesterol, .87 mg sodium

Per tablespoon of mayonnaise: 84 calories, .30 g protein, .07 g carbohydrate, 9 g total fat, 12 mg cholesterol, 11 mg sodium

Chile con Queso

- 2 tablespoons butter or margarine
- 1 large onion, chopped
- 1 cup prepared hot salsa
- 1 pound processed American cheese, shredded
- ½ cup buttermilk or plain yogurt
- 3 medium-size bell peppers (red, green, yellow, or a combination), seeded and cut into 1-inch-wide strips
- 1 bag (12 oz.) corn chips

In a 2- to 3-quart pan (suitable for serving, if desired), melt butter over medium-high heat. Add onion and cook, stirring often, until soft (5 to 7 minutes). Add salsa and bring to a boil; remove from heat. Add cheese, stirring until melted. Blend in buttermilk. Return pan to low heat and stir just until heated through (do not boil).

Keep sauce warm over a candle or on a warming tray. Serve with bell pepper strips and corn chips to dip into sauce. Makes 10 to 12 appetizer servings.

Per serving: 342 calories, 11 g protein, 19 g carbohydrates, 24 g total fat, 41 mg cholesterol, 880 mg sodium

Shrimp with Tart Dipping Sauce

- 35 chives (about 7 inches long *each*)
- 1 pound medium-size shrimp (31 to 35 per lb.), cooked, shelled, and deveined
  Tart Dipping Sauce (recipe follows)

Tie a chive around center of each shrimp. Prepare Tart Dipping Sauce and pour into a small bowl. Arrange shrimp on a platter and offer sauce alongside. If made ahead, cover and refrigerate for up to 4 hours. Makes about 8 appetizer servings.

Tart Dipping Sauce. Stir together ¼ cup *each* **dry white wine** and **white wine vinegar**, 1 tablespoon *each* minced **shallots** and **chives**, and ½ teaspoon **pepper.**

Per serving of shrimp: 48 calories, 10 g protein, .16 g carbohydrate, .72 g total fat, 65 mg cholesterol, 96 mg sodium

Per teaspoon of sauce: 2 calories, 0 g protein, .20 g carbohydrate, 0 g total fat, 0 mg cholesterol, .13 mg sodium

Scallops with Shallot Butter

- 18 sea scallops (about 1 lb.)
- ⅓ cup butter or margarine, at room temperature
- ⅓ cup minced shallots
- 1 or 2 cloves garlic, minced or pressed
- 2 tablespoons minced parsley
  Salt and pepper
  Lemon wedges

Rinse scallops and pat dry; arrange in 6 natural scallop shells or 5- to 6-inch shallow baking dishes. Mix butter, shallots, garlic, and parsley. Dot scallops with shallot butter and season with salt and pepper to taste. Set shells in a shallow rimmed 10- by 15-inch baking pan.

Bake on top shelf of a 500° oven until scallops are opaque in thickest part when cut (about 10 minutes). Garnish with lemon. Makes 6 first-course servings.

Per serving: 166 calories, 14 g protein, 4 g carbohydrates, 11 g total fat, 55 mg cholesterol, 227 mg sodium

Quail Eggs with Toasted Pepper

- 1½ dozen quail eggs
- 2 teaspoons salt
- 2 tablespoons cracked pepper

Place quail eggs in a 1½- to 2-quart pan; cover with water. Bring to a boil over high heat; reduce heat and simmer, uncovered, for 6 minutes.

Meanwhile, in a small frying pan over medium heat, combine salt and pepper. Heat, stirring often, until salt is pale gold (about 5 minutes).

Serve eggs warm; or, to serve cold, let cool in cold water, then drain and refrigerate until thoroughly chilled or for up to 3 days.

Spoon pepper mixture into a small bowl. Serve eggs in a basket. To eat, peel eggs and dip into pepper mixture. Makes 6 appetizer servings.

Per serving: 47 calories, 4 g protein, 1 g carbohydrate, 3 g total fat, 228 mg cholesterol, 550 mg sodium

Main-dish Salads

Festively garnished with orange zest,
this chicken breast can be hickory smoked right in your own oven
in less than half an hour. Complete Smoked Chicken Breast Salad (recipe on
facing page) with mixed greens and an orange-flavored vinaigrette.

A crisp, colorful salad makes a spectacular presentation, yet usually takes only minutes to compose. And it's the kind of dish that many prefer nowadays: fresh, light, healthy, and casual. In this chapter, we've introduced such hearty ingredients as sliced beef, shredded chicken, and delicate seafood morsels to transform garden-variety salads into full entrées. Whether you choose a cool, no-cook salad or a warming winter one, you'll find it easy, quick to create, and satisfying.

Smoked Chicken Breast Salad

(Pictured on facing page)

 PREPARATION TIME **15** MINUTES **25** MINUTES COOKING TIME

Sweet-tart oranges—in the garnishes and in the vinaigrette—accent mellow oven-smoked chicken breasts in this main-dish salad. Toasted pecans add appetizing crunch. For a light but satisfying menu, accompany with crusty whole wheat French bread and a glass of white Zinfandel.

- 3 **tablespoons liquid smoke**
- 2 **whole chicken breasts (about 1 lb. *each*), skinned, boned, and split**
  Orange Vinaigrette (recipe follows)
- 1 **tablespoon butter or margarine**
- ¾ **cup pecan halves**
- 1½ **quarts mixed salad greens, such as butter and romaine lettuce and watercress, washed and crisped**
  Orange zest
  Orange wedges

Pour liquid smoke into a 5- to 6-quart pan. Set a rack in pan. Arrange chicken breasts in a single layer on rack and cover pan tightly. Bake in a 350° oven until chicken is white in center when slashed (20 to 25 minutes). If made ahead, let cool; then cover and refrigerate for up to 2 days.

Meanwhile, prepare Orange Vinaigrette; set aside.

In a medium-size frying pan, melt butter over low heat. Add pecans and stir until nuts are slightly darkened and have a toasted flavor (about 6 minutes). Drain on paper towels.

Arrange salad greens on 4 dinner plates and sprinkle with pecans.

Cut each chicken breast into ¼-inch-thick slanting slices. Arrange on plates beside greens. Spoon dressing over greens and chicken. Garnish with orange zest and orange wedges. Makes 4 servings.

Orange Vinaigrette. Mix ¼ cup **orange juice**, 2 tablespoons *each* **white wine vinegar** and **salad oil**, 1 tablespoon thinly slivered or shredded **orange peel** (colored part only), 2 teaspoons *each* **honey** and **Dijon mustard,** and ½ teaspoon **coarsely ground pepper.**

Per serving: 441 calories, 42 g protein, 11 g carbohydrates, 26 g total fat, 105 mg cholesterol, 225 mg sodium

Chicken Salad with Sesame Dressing

PREPARATION TIME **40** MINUTES

Crisp celery, juicy kiwi fruit, and creamy avocado bring three delicious contrasts of texture and flavor to tender shredded chicken. A lemony toasted sesame seed dressing unites all.

Sesame Dressing (recipe follows)
- 3 **quarts bite-size pieces leaf lettuce, washed and crisped**
- 4 **large kiwi fruit**
- 1 **large avocado**
- 2 **cups shredded cooked chicken**
- 1 **cup thinly sliced celery**
- ⅓ **cup thinly sliced green onions (including tops)**

Prepare Sesame Dressing; set aside.

Spread lettuce in a wide salad bowl. Peel kiwi fruit and thinly slice crosswise. Pit, peel, and slice avocado. Arrange kiwi fruit, chicken, avocado, celery, and onions over lettuce. Pour dressing over salad and mix lightly. Makes 4 or 5 servings.

Sesame Dressing. Heat ⅓ cup **salad oil** in a small frying pan over low heat. Add 3 tablespoons **sesame seeds** and cook, stirring often, until seeds are golden (about 5 minutes). Remove from heat and let cool for 10 minutes. Stir in ½ teaspoon *each* grated **lemon peel** and **dry mustard,** ¼ cup **lemon juice,** and 1 tablespoon *each* **sugar** and **soy sauce.** Season with **salt** to taste.

Per serving: 437 calories, 21 g protein, 26 g carbohydrates, 30 g total fat, 50 mg cholesterol, 300 mg sodium

Curry & Fruit Chicken Salad

PREPARATION TIME **30** MINUTES

This chicken and fruit salad showcases a combination of bold and spicy ingredients derived from East Indian cuisine. Choose either sour cream or yogurt as the base for the dressing.

Dill-Curry Dressing (recipe follows)
- 1 **medium-size red apple**
- 3 **cups cooked chicken, cut into ½-inch-wide strips**
- 2 **cups thinly sliced celery**
- ¾ **cup dry-roasted salted peanuts**
- ½ **cup raisins**
- 1 **small pineapple (about 3 lbs.)**
- 8 **to 10 large lettuce leaves, washed and crisped**
- 2 **tablespoons minced candied ginger (optional)**

Prepare Dill-Curry Dressing and refrigerate.

Core apple and cut lengthwise into thin slivers. Combine apple, chicken, celery, ½ cup of the peanuts, raisins, and dressing; mix gently.

Preparing Salad Greens

If you keep greens washed and crisped, you can create winning salads in the wink of an eye.

To prepare the greens, remove and discard the core, separate the leaves, and plunge them into a quantity of cold water so that dirt floats free. Drain the greens well or whirl them in a salad spinner. Wrap them loosely in paper towels, place in a plastic bag, and refrigerate for at least 30 minutes. Enclosed in a plastic bag, most salad greens can be held in the refrigerator for up to 2 days—iceberg and romaine lettuce will last for as long as 5 days.

Peel and slice pineapple. Arrange lettuce leaves on 4 or 5 dinner plates; lay pineapple on lettuce and top with chicken salad. Sprinkle salads with remaining ¼ cup peanuts and, if desired, candied ginger. Makes 4 or 5 servings.

Dill-Curry Dressing. Mix 1 cup **sour cream** or plain yogurt, 2 tablespoons **lemon juice,** 1½ teaspoons **curry powder,** and ½ teaspoon **dill weed.**

Per serving: 527 calories, 33 g protein, 43 g carbohydrates, 28 g total fat, 96 mg cholesterol, 337 mg sodium

San Diego Salad

PREPARATION TIME **25** MINUTES

Befitting a salad from San Diego, this colorful composition displays ingredients popular in Mexican cuisine: chicken, cheese, oranges, avocado, tortilla chips, and, in the creamy dressing, cumin and salsa.

Creamy Cumin Dressing (recipe follows)
- 1 **head romaine lettuce, washed and crisped**
- 2 **whole cooked chicken breasts (about 1 lb. *each*), skinned, boned, and split**
- 3 **to 4 ounces jack cheese, cut into bite-size strips**
- 12 **thin slices salami**
- 2 **oranges, peeled and sliced**
- 1 **avocado**
  Pitted ripe olives
  Tortilla chips

Prepare Creamy Cumin Dressing; set aside.

Arrange large outer lettuce leaves on 4 dinner plates. Finely chop inner leaves and arrange over whole leaves. Cut chicken into strips; place on lettuce. Add cheese, salami, and orange slices. Pit, peel, and slice avocado; add to salads. Garnish with olives and tortilla chips. Offer dressing at the table to add to taste. Makes 4 servings.

Creamy Cumin Dressing. Mix ⅓ cup *each* **sour cream** and **mayonnaise,** 1½ tablespoons **lemon juice,** ¼ teaspoon *each* **dry mustard** and **garlic salt,** ½ teaspoon **ground cumin,** and 3 tablespoons canned **green** or red **chile salsa.** Makes about 1 cup.

Per serving of salad: 511 calories, 49 g protein, 17 g carbohydrates, 28 g total fat, 133 mg cholesterol, 644 mg sodium

Per tablespoon of dressing: 44 calories, .19 g protein, .62 g carbohydrate, 5 g total fat, 5 mg cholesterol, 74 mg sodium

Chicken & Avocado Salad

PREPARATION TIME **15** MINUTES   **10** MINUTES COOKING TIME

Classic salad makings—shredded chicken breast, sliced avocado, chopped hard-cooked egg, crumbled bacon, and crisp romaine—are tossed together in this one-bowl supper with a blue cheese vinaigrette.

> 6 **slices bacon**
> **Cheese Dressing (recipe follows)**
> 3 **quarts bite-size pieces romaine lettuce, washed and crisped**
> 3 **cups shredded cooked chicken breasts**
> 1 **avocado**
> 1 **hard-cooked egg, chopped**

In a wide frying pan, cook bacon over medium heat until crisp. Lift out, drain, and crumble; set aside.

Prepare Cheese Dressing; set aside.

Place lettuce in a large salad bowl. Mound chicken over lettuce. Pit, peel, and slice avocado. Scatter avocado, egg, and bacon over chicken. Pour dressing over salad. Mix lightly. Makes 6 servings.

Cheese Dressing. Mix ½ cup **olive oil** or salad oil, ¼ cup **white wine vinegar**, 1 teaspoon **Dijon mustard,** ¼ teaspoon **pepper,** and ¼ cup crumbled **blue-veined cheese.**

Per serving: 420 calories, 29 g protein, 6 g carbohydrates, 32 g total fat, 116 mg cholesterol, 281 mg sodium

Sesame-Plum Chicken Salad

PREPARATION TIME **20** MINUTES

Sweet and pungent Chinese plum sauce, blended with crushed pineapple and toasted sesame seeds, makes an intriguing dressing for chicken salad.

> **Sesame Plum Sauce (recipe follows)**
> 1½ **quarts shredded lettuce**
> 3 **cups shredded cooked chicken**
> 2 **green onions (including tops)**
> **Fresh cilantro (coriander) sprigs**

Prepare Sesame Plum Sauce; set aside.

Spread lettuce on a serving platter. Mound chicken over lettuce; spoon sauce over chicken. Cut onions into 2-inch lengths, then into thin lengthwise shreds. Garnish salad with onions and cilantro. Makes 4 servings.

Sesame Plum Sauce. In a small frying pan, toast 2 tablespoons **sesame seeds** over medium heat, shaking pan frequently, until golden (about 5 minutes). Drain 1 can (8 oz.) **crushed pineapple,** discarding liquid. Mix pineapple, ½ cup canned **plum sauce,** 1½ tablespoons **sugar,** 1 tablespoon **white vinegar,** and toasted sesame seeds.

Per serving: 317 calories, 33 g protein, 23 g carbohydrates, 10 g total fat, 95 mg cholesterol, 107 mg sodium

Szechwan Chicken Salad

PREPARATION TIME **20** MINUTES   **10** MINUTES COOKING TIME

Won ton skins, cut into strips and crisply fried, accent this Chinese chicken salad. Peanut butter combines with hot chili oil to season the piquant dressing.

> 2 **tablespoons creamy peanut butter**
> 3 **tablespoons soy sauce**
> ¼ **cup rice vinegar**
> 2 **teaspoons sugar**
> **About ¼ teaspoon hot chili oil or ground red pepper (cayenne)**
> 2 **tablespoons sesame seeds**
> **Salad oil**
> 6 **won ton skins (about 3 inches square), cut into ¼-inch-wide strips**
> 2 **quarts finely shredded iceberg lettuce**
> 2 **green onions (including tops), thinly sliced**
> 2 **to 3 cups shredded cooked chicken**
> 2 **tablespoons chopped fresh cilantro (coriander)**

Place peanut butter in a small bowl; with a fork, smoothly mix in soy sauce, a little at a time, until well blended. Stir in vinegar and sugar; season with chili oil to taste.

In a small frying pan, toast sesame seeds over medium heat, shaking pan frequently, until golden (about 5 minutes); set sesame seeds aside.

Pour salad oil into pan to a depth of about ¼ inch, increase heat to medium-high, and add won ton strips, about half at a time. Cook, stirring, until lightly browned (1½ to 2 minutes). With a slotted spoon, lift out strips and drain on paper towels.

Place lettuce in a large salad bowl; top with onions, chicken, and dressing. Sprinkle with sesame seeds, fried won ton strips, and cilantro. Mix lightly. Makes 4 to 6 servings.

Per serving: 276 calories, 25 g protein, 12 g carbohydrates, 15 g total fat, 69 mg cholesterol, 609 mg sodium

Grecian Chicken Salad Plates

PREPARATION TIME **30** MINUTES

As carefree as an Aegean breeze, this summertime menu offers rice-stuffed grape leaves, deli-roasted or barbecued chicken, and a Greek salad. Serve with sesame seed bread and chilled dry white or fruity rosé wine.

1 jar (6 oz.) marinated artichoke hearts
1 teaspoon grated lemon peel
1 tablespoon lemon juice
1 clove garlic, minced or pressed
½ teaspoon dry oregano
2 tablespoons chopped fresh mint or
2 teaspoons dry mint
3 tablespoons olive oil
1 tablespoon drained capers
1 small cucumber
1 head romaine lettuce, washed and crisped
2 cups cherry tomatoes, cut in half
1 yellow or green bell pepper, seeded and cut into thin strips
1 cooked (rotisseried or barbecued) whole chicken (2 to 2½ lbs.), cut into quarters
¼ pound feta cheese, crumbled
Greek olives
1 small can (6½ oz.) stuffed grape leaves, drained

Drain artichokes, reserving marinade in a small bowl; set artichokes aside. To marinade add lemon peel, lemon juice, garlic, oregano, and mint; beat in oil with a whisk until well combined. Stir in capers. Set dressing aside.

Peel cucumber; cut in half lengthwise. Scoop out and discard seeds. Slice each half crosswise into ⅛-inch-thick slices. Set aside large outer lettuce leaves; tear inner leaves into bite-size pieces.

Combine cucumber, torn lettuce leaves, tomatoes, bell pepper, and artichoke hearts. Reserve 2 tablespoons of the dressing. Mix salad lightly with remaining dressing.

Coarsely sliver large lettuce leaves and arrange on 4 dinner plates. Place a chicken quarter on one side of each plate; mound salad mixture on other side. Sprinkle salad with cheese. Drizzle chicken with reserved dressing and garnish each salad with olives and stuffed grape leaves. Makes 4 servings.

Per serving: 604 calories, 43 g protein, 14 g carbohydrates, 42 g total fat, 135 mg cholesterol, 1041 mg sodium

Curried Turkey Salad with Papaya

PREPARATION TIME **30** MINUTES

Fanned out from a mound of curried and cashew-strewn turkey salad, spears of papaya and romaine lettuce offer both decorative looks and delicious taste.

Curry Dressing (recipe follows)
3 cups diced cooked turkey or chicken
1 cup thinly sliced celery
½ cup thinly sliced green onions (including tops)
Salt and ground red pepper (cayenne)
8 to 12 large romaine lettuce leaves, washed and crisped
2 large papayas, peeled, seeded, and sliced lengthwise
¼ cup roasted salted cashews
1 lemon, cut into wedges

Prepare Curry Dressing; set aside.

Combine turkey, celery, and onions; mix lightly with dressing. Season with salt and red pepper to taste.

Arrange lettuce leaves on 4 dinner plates. Mound turkey salad on each plate. Arrange papaya slices alongside. Sprinkle cashews over salad. Offer lemon to squeeze over salad and fruit. Makes 4 servings.

Curry Dressing. Mix 1 cup **sour cream;** 2 tablespoons minced **candied ginger;** 1 tablespoon *each* **curry powder, lemon juice,** and **Dijon mustard;** and ½ teaspoon **cumin seeds.**

Per serving: 477 calories, 37 g protein, 35 g carbohydrates, 22 g total fat, 107 mg cholesterol, 318 mg sodium

Turkey, Red Pepper & Blue Cheese Salad

Follow directions for Curried Turkey Salad with Papaya, but omit Curry Dressing, celery, ground red pepper, papayas, cashews, and lemon.

For dressing, mix ½ cup *each* **sour cream** and **mayonnaise,** 1 tablespoon *each* **prepared horseradish** and **lemon juice,** and ⅛ teaspoon **pepper.**

For salad, combine turkey, onions, and 1 large **red bell pepper,** seeded and chopped. Mix lightly with ½ cup crumbled **blue-veined cheese** and dressing. Season with salt to taste. Arrange lettuce leaves and turkey salad as directed. Sprinkle with ½ cup **dry-roasted peanuts.**

A cool candidate for warm summer weather,
Cashew, Shrimp & Pea Salad (recipe on page 21) demands no
cooking and very little preparation time. Its creamy dill dressing adds a
Scandinavian touch. Serve with iced tea and crisp rye flatbread.

Pasta & Rice

From its sprig of fresh basil to its bed of linguine,
Pasta with Shrimp in Tomato Cream (recipe on facing page)
makes a showy presentation. Complement the succulent shrimp with a crisp
salad, crusty rolls, and a chilled blush wine, such as white Zinfandel.

In bygone days, a pasta dinner meant hours in the kitchen, patiently stirring a slow and complex spaghetti sauce. But the recent revival of interest in pasta, both fresh and dry, has revealed the previously well-kept secret that many tantalizing sauces take only minutes to create. And, along with pasta, rice offers another mouth-watering vehicle for today's fresh, light, and richly flavored sauces. Perfect choices for a hurry-up meal, both pasta and rice cook in about as much time as it takes to toss the salad and warm up a crusty loaf of bread.

Pasta with Shrimp in Tomato Cream

(Pictured on facing page)

PREPARATION TIME   COOKING TIME

Sun-dried tomatoes join shrimp, basil, and cream in an elegant sauce for linguine. You'll need oil-packed dried tomatoes to create the full flavor of the rosy sauce.

- ⅓ **cup dried tomatoes packed in oil, drained (reserve oil) and slivered**
- 1 **clove garlic, minced or pressed**
- 1 **pound large (31 to 35 per lb.) shrimp, shelled and deveined**
- ¼ **cup thinly sliced green onions (including tops)**
- 1½ **tablespoons chopped fresh basil leaves or 1 teaspoon dry basil**
- ¼ **teaspoon white pepper**
- 1 **cup regular-strength chicken broth**
- ¾ **cup dry vermouth**
- 1 **cup whipping cream**
- 10 **ounces linguine**
  Fresh basil sprigs (optional)
  Grated Parmesan cheese

Measure 2 tablespoons of the oil from tomatoes; set tomatoes aside. Heat oil in a wide frying pan over medium-high heat. When oil is hot, add garlic and shrimp. Cook, stirring often, until shrimp are opaque in center when cut (about 6 minutes). Lift out and set aside.

Add onions, chopped basil, tomatoes, pepper, broth, vermouth, and cream to pan. Boil over high heat, stirring occasionally, until reduced to about 1½ cups (about 10 minutes). Return shrimp to pan and stir just until heated through.

Meanwhile, in a 4- to 5-quart pan, bring 3 quarts water to a boil over high heat. Add linguine; let water return to a boil and cook just until *al dente* (about 8 minutes). Or cook according to package directions. Drain linguine. Arrange on 4 dinner plates and spoon sauce over. Garnish with basil, if desired. Offer cheese to add to taste. Makes 4 servings.

Per serving: 592 calories, 30 g protein, 61 g carbohydrates, 24 g total fat, 197 mg cholesterol, 469 mg sodium

Stir-fried Pasta with Shrimp

PREPARATION TIME COOKING TIME

This cross-cultural dinner for two merges a Chinese technique with the flavors of Italy. Complete a delightful short-order menu with crusty bread and a full-bodied white wine.

- 6 **ounces linguine**
- 2 **tablespoons olive oil**
- 1 **small onion, cut into bite-size chunks**
- 1 **medium-size green bell pepper, seeded and cut into bite-size chunks**
- ¼ **to ½ teaspoon crushed red pepper**
- ½ **to 1 teaspoon dry oregano**
- 2 **ounces Chinese pea pods (also called snow or sugar peas), stem ends and strings removed**
- 1 **to 2 tablespoons butter or margarine**
- ¾ **pound small cooked shrimp**
  About ½ cup grated Parmesan cheese

In a 3- to 4-quart pan, bring 1½ quarts water to a boil over high heat. Add linguine when you begin to stir-fry vegetables.

Heat oil in a wok or wide frying pan over high heat. When oil is hot, add onion, bell pepper, and crushed red pepper and oregano to taste. Stir-fry until vegetables are just tender (about 5 minutes).

Add pea pods and butter to taste. Continue to stir-fry until butter is melted (about 1 minute). Add shrimp and stir just until heated through. Remove pan from heat.

Cook pasta just until *al dente* (about 8 minutes). Or cook according to package directions. Drain pasta and arrange on a warm platter. Spoon shrimp mixture over and sprinkle with cheese to taste. Makes 2 servings.

Per serving: 855 calories, 62 g protein, 72 g carbohydrates, 34 g total fat, 302 mg cholesterol, 732 mg sodium

Lemon Scallops with Fusilli

PREPARATION TIME **8** MINUTES   **10** MINUTES COOKING TIME

Gently cook tiny scallops to perfection in a light, buttery wine sauce; then catch the sauce's good flavor in the twists and turns of spiral-shaped fusilli (also called rotelle). Offer broccoli spears alongside for contrast.

- 8 ounces fusilli, rotelle, or other medium-size fancy-shaped pasta
- ¼ cup dry white wine
- ¼ teaspoon grated lemon peel
- 2 tablespoons lemon juice
- 2 green onions (including tops), thinly sliced
- 2 tablespoons drained capers
- 1 teaspoon dry rosemary
- ½ teaspoon dry basil
- 2 cloves garlic, minced or pressed
- ½ pound bay scallops, rinsed and patted dry
- ¼ cup butter or margarine
  Chopped parsley

In a 4- to 5-quart pan, bring 2 quarts water to a boil over high heat. Add fusilli; let water return to a boil and cook just until *al dente* (8 to 10 minutes). Or cook according to package directions.

Meanwhile, in a wide frying pan, combine wine, lemon peel, lemon juice, onions, capers, rosemary, basil, and garlic. Boil over high heat, stirring often, until liquid is reduced by half. Add scallops, stirring just until coated with lemon mixture and heated through (about 30 seconds). Remove pan from heat and add butter all at once, stirring constantly to incorporate.

Drain pasta and add to sauce. Lift with 2 forks until coated. Sprinkle with parsley. Makes 3 or 4 servings.

Per serving: 372 calories, 17 g protein, 46 g carbohydrates, 13 g total fat, 52 mg cholesterol, 322 mg sodium

Pasta & Smoked Salmon

PREPARATION TIME **5** MINUTES   **15** MINUTES COOKING TIME

Smoke fresh salmon in just 10 to 12 minutes in your oven, then serve it warm over linguine, bathed in a tangy cream sauce. Add a cucumber and butter lettuce salad with a lemon vinaigrette dressing.

- 3 tablespoons liquid smoke
- ¾ pound salmon fillet, skinned and cut into ½-inch-wide strips
- 12 ounces linguine or spaghetti
- 2 tablespoons white wine vinegar
- ½ cup finely chopped onion
- 1 cup whipping cream
- ¾ cup dry white wine
- 1 tablespoon Dijon mustard
- ¼ cup grated Parmesan cheese
  Parsley sprigs
  Salt and pepper

Pour liquid smoke into a 5- to 6-quart pan. Set a rack in pan. Arrange salmon in a single layer on rack and cover pan tightly. Bake in a 350° oven until fish is opaque in thickest part when cut (10 to 12 minutes). Set aside.

Meanwhile, in a 4- to 5-quart pan, bring 3 quarts water to a boil over high heat. Add linguine; let water return to a boil and cook just until *al dente* (about 10 minutes). Or cook according to package directions.

Meanwhile, combine vinegar and onion in a wide frying pan. Boil over high heat until vinegar has evaporated (about 2 minutes). Add cream, wine, and mustard. Boil, stirring often, until sauce is reduced to 1¾ cups. Drain linguine and add to cream mixture; lift with 2 forks until coated.

Arrange linguine on 4 dinner plates; sprinkle each serving with 1 tablespoon of the cheese. Arrange salmon over linguine. Garnish with parsley. Offer salt and pepper to add to taste. Makes 4 servings.

Per serving: 715 calories, 33 g protein, 70 g carbohydrates, 33 g total fat, 103 mg cholesterol, 292 mg sodium

Pasta alla Puttanesca

PREPARATION TIME **15** MINUTES   **25** MINUTES COOKING TIME

At the spur of the moment, you can toss together this pasta from ingredients you're likely to have on hand in the pantry and refrigerator. In the piquant parlance of Italian cuisine, its name means "harlot's pasta."

- Tomato Sauce (recipe follows)
- 8 ounces linguine or vermicelli
- ½ cup oil-cured black ripe olives, rinsed, patted dry, and pitted (if desired)
- 1 can (2 oz.) flat anchovy fillets, rinsed, patted dry, and diced
- 1 tablespoon drained capers
- 1 can (6½ oz.) chunk light tuna packed in water, drained
- ⅓ cup chopped parsley

Prepare Tomato Sauce. Meanwhile, in a 4- to 5-quart pan, bring 2 quarts water to a boil over high heat. Add linguine; let water return to a boil and cook just until *al dente* (8 to 10 minutes). Or cook according to package directions.

To sauce add olives, anchovies, capers, tuna, and parsley. Cook, stirring occasionally, until heated through.

Drain linguine and arrange on a warm platter. Spoon sauce over. Makes 4 servings.

Tomato Sauce. In a 2½- to 3-quart pan, combine 2 tablespoons **olive oil;** 1 small **onion,** chopped; 3 cloves **garlic,** minced or pressed; ½ teaspoon *each* **dry basil** and **oregano;** and ¼ teaspoon **crushed red pepper.** Cook over medium-high heat, stirring often, until onion is lightly browned (6 to 8 minutes). Add 1 large can (28 oz.) **pear-shaped tomatoes with basil;** break up tomatoes with a spoon. Bring to a boil over high heat and cook, stirring often, until sauce is reduced to about 2 cups (about 15 minutes).

Per serving: 473 calories, 23 g protein, 56 g carbohydrates, 19 g total fat, 31 mg cholesterol, 1495 mg sodium

Chicken Pasta Italiano

PREPARATION TIME **12** MINUTES   **25** MINUTES COOKING TIME

Choose the reddest, ripest tomatoes for this zesty, fresh-tasting pasta sauce that also offers strips of chicken, crisp bacon bits, and a generous amount of garlic.

- ¼ **pound sliced bacon, chopped**
- 4 **cloves garlic, minced or pressed**
- ¾ **pound skinned, boned chicken breast, cut into ¼-inch-wide strips**
- 4 **medium-size tomatoes, seeded and chopped**
- ½ **cup dry sherry or regular-strength chicken broth**
- 1 **tablespoon Italian seasoning or ¾ teaspoon *each* dry basil, oregano, thyme, and marjoram**
- ⅛ **teaspoon ground red pepper (cayenne)**
- 6 **ounces spaghetti**
- ½ **cup grated Parmesan cheese**

In a wide frying pan, cook bacon over medium heat until crisp. Lift out, drain, and set aside. Discard all but 2 tablespoons of the drippings.

Add garlic and chicken to pan. Cook over high heat, stirring, until meat is lightly browned (about 3 minutes). Remove chicken from pan and set aside.

Add tomatoes, sherry, Italian seasoning, and red pepper to pan; boil over high heat until most of the liquid has evaporated (about 10 minutes).

Meanwhile, in a 4- to 5-quart pan, bring 2 quarts water to a boil over high heat. Add spaghetti; let water return to a boil and cook just until *al dente* (10 to 12 minutes). Or cook according to package directions.

Return chicken to tomato mixture; stir until heated through. Drain spaghetti and arrange on a warm platter. Spoon chicken mixture over and sprinkle with bacon. Offer cheese to add to taste. Makes 2 or 3 servings.

Per serving: 574 calories, 44 g protein, 56 g carbohydrates, 18 g total fat, 92 mg cholesterol, 568 mg sodium

To Microwave: Place bacon in a 9- to 10-inch microwave-safe dish; cover lightly with a paper towel. Microwave on **HIGH (100%)** for 6 to 7 minutes, stirring once or twice, until bacon is crisp and browned. Lift out, drain, and set aside; discard all but about 1 tablespoon of the drippings. Stir in garlic and chicken. Cover and microwave on **HIGH (100%)** for 4 to 5 minutes, stirring once, until chicken is opaque throughout. Lift out chicken and set aside.

Add tomatoes to dish. Reduce sherry to ¼ cup and add to tomatoes with Italian seasoning and red pepper. Microwave, uncovered, on **HIGH (100%)** for about 15 minutes, stirring 2 or 3 times, until tomatoes are soft.

Meanwhile, cook spaghetti as directed. Stir chicken into tomato sauce and microwave, uncovered, on **HIGH (100%)** for 1 to 2 minutes or until heated through. Serve as directed.

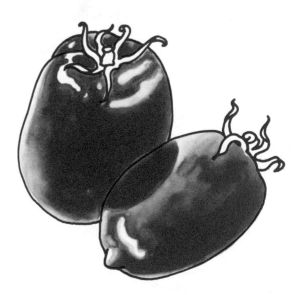

Vermicelli with Chicken Livers

PREPARATION TIME **10** MINUTES   **20** MINUTES COOKING TIME

Pasta with a savory sauce of sautéed chicken livers is sometimes known as Spaghetti Caruso. Like the great singer, you may burst into song when you taste this magnificent, yet easy, rendition.

> 1 tablespoon butter or margarine
> 1 tablespoon olive oil
> 2 slices (about 2 oz.) pancetta or bacon, diced
> 1 pound chicken livers, cut in half
> 1 medium-size onion, thinly sliced
> ¼ pound mushrooms, sliced
> 1 clove garlic, minced or pressed
> 1 teaspoon herbes de Provence or Italian seasoning; or ¼ teaspoon *each* dry basil, oregano, thyme, and marjoram
> 1 can (8 oz.) tomato sauce
> 2 tablespoons tomato paste
> ½ cup dry red wine
> 8 ounces vermicelli or spaghettini
> Salt and pepper
> Chopped parsley
> Grated Parmesan cheese

In a wide frying pan, melt butter with oil over medium heat. Add pancetta and cook, stirring often, until crisp and lightly browned; with a slotted spoon, lift out pancetta, reserving drippings in pan, and set aside.

Add chicken livers, about half at a time, to pan. Increase heat to medium-high and cook until well browned on all sides; remove from pan, reserving drippings. Add onion, mushrooms, garlic, and herbs to pan. Cook, stirring often, until onion is soft (about 5 minutes). Stir in tomato sauce, tomato paste, and wine. Reduce heat to low and simmer, uncovered, for about 5 minutes.

Meanwhile, in a 4- to 5-quart pan, bring 2 quarts water to a boil over high heat. Add vermicelli; let water return to a boil and cook just until *al dente* (10 to 12 minutes). Or cook according to package directions.

Add chicken livers and pancetta to tomato sauce; cook just until heated through. Season with salt and pepper to taste.

Drain vermicelli and serve with sauce spooned over. Sprinkle with parsley. Offer cheese to add to taste. Makes 4 servings.

Per serving: 530 calories, 31 g protein, 57 g carbohydrates, 20 g total fat, 516 mg cholesterol, 632 mg sodium

Turkey Spaghetti Marinara

PREPARATION TIME **10** MINUTES   **30** MINUTES COOKING TIME

The rich, traditional flavor of this superb spaghetti sauce can be achieved in just 30 minutes. And the result has a welcome lightness because the sauce is made with lean ground turkey. Spoon it over spaghetti or fresh noodles, such as tagliarini.

> 1 tablespoon olive oil
> 1 small onion, finely chopped
> ½ cup finely chopped green bell pepper
> 1 medium-size carrot, finely shredded
> 3 mushrooms, thinly sliced
> 1 tablespoon chopped parsley
> 1 clove garlic, minced or pressed
> 1 teaspoon dry basil
> ½ teaspoon *each* dry rosemary and oregano
> 1 pound ground turkey
> 1 large can (28 oz.) pear-shaped tomatoes
> 1 small can (6 oz.) tomato paste
> ⅓ cup dry red wine
> 1 bay leaf
> 8 to 12 ounces spaghetti
> Salt and pepper
> Grated Parmesan cheese

In a wide frying pan, combine oil, onion, bell pepper, carrot, mushrooms, parsley, garlic, basil, rosemary, and oregano. Cook over medium-high heat, stirring often, until onion is soft (about 5 minutes). Crumble turkey into pan and cook, stirring often, until turkey is lightly browned. Add tomatoes (break up with a spoon) and their liquid, tomato paste, wine, and bay leaf; bring to a boil. Adjust heat so mixture boils gently and cook, stirring occasionally, until sauce is thickened (about 20 minutes).

Meanwhile, in a 4- to 5-quart pan, bring 2 to 3 quarts water to a boil over high heat. Add spaghetti; let water return to a boil and cook just until *al dente* (12 to 15 minutes). Or cook according to package directions.

Season sauce with salt and pepper to taste. Discard bay leaf. Drain spaghetti and serve with marinara sauce spooned over. Offer cheese to add to taste. Makes 4 to 6 servings.

Per serving: 419 calories, 23 g protein, 57 g carbohydrates, 11 g total fat, 51 mg cholesterol, 517 mg sodium

Occasionally, Italians enjoy a dish of creamy
rice instead of pasta—and one taste of Mushroom Risotto
with Italian Sausage Sauce (recipe on page 29) will convince you of its
special appeal. Offer it with hot garlic bread.

Convenient Sauces

When you're cooking in a hurry, you learn to appreciate those little touches of culinary artistry that make all the difference to appetizing appeal. Such details as a dollop of pesto on a plump tomato slice or a daub of fresh herb butter on an ear of sweet corn can make a more eloquent impression than some dishes requiring hours of preparation. Take a few minutes now to cache away the following flavorful sauces, and they'll pay off handsomely later on when you need a little last-minute magic.

Toasted Almond Skordalia

- ⅓ cup whole unblanched almonds
- 2 egg yolks
- 2 cloves garlic, minced or pressed
- 1½ tablespoons lemon juice
- ½ teaspoon sugar
- 1 to 4 tablespoons dry white wine
- 1 cup olive oil or salad oil
  Salt

Spread almonds in a shallow 9-inch baking pan. Bake in a 350° oven until nuts are golden under skin when broken (about 8 minutes); let cool. Whirl in a blender or food processor until finely ground; set aside.

In blender or food processor, whirl egg yolks, garlic, lemon juice, sugar, and 1 tablespoon of the wine until blended. With motor running, pour in oil in a slow, steady stream. Stir in almonds. For a thinner consistency (to serve as a dip), add more wine. Season with salt to taste. If made ahead, cover and refrigerate for up to 2 days.

Serve as a dip for raw or blanched vegetables or as a sauce for grilled fish or chicken. Makes about 1½ cups.

Per tablespoon: 99 calories, .63 g protein, .71 g carbohydrate, 10 g total fat, 23 mg cholesterol, 1 mg sodium

Savory Cream Dip

- 1 cup sour cream or plain yogurt
- ¼ cup chopped fresh basil, dill, fennel, or thyme leaves
  Salt and pepper

Mix sour cream and basil until well blended. Season with salt and pepper to taste. Cover and refrigerate for at least an hour or for up to 2 weeks.

Serve as a salad dressing or dip for fresh vegetables, or as a sauce for fish. Makes about 1 cup.

Per tablespoon: 31 calories, .49 g protein, .78 g carbohydrate, 3 g total fat, 6 mg cholesterol, 8 mg sodium

Fresh Herb Mayonnaise

- 1 cup mayonnaise
- 2 teaspoons lemon juice
- ½ cup chopped fresh basil, dill, marjoram, oregano, or savory leaves; or ¼ cup tarragon leaves

Smoothly mix mayonnaise, lemon juice, and basil. Cover and refrigerate for at least 8 hours or for up to a month.

Serve as a dressing for green salad or sliced tomatoes, as a dip for artichokes, as a spread for roast beef or turkey sandwiches, or to make deviled eggs or tuna or chicken salad. Makes about 1 cup.

Per tablespoon: 100 calories, .23 g protein, .75 g carbohydrate, 11 g total fat, 8 mg cholesterol, 78 mg sodium

Pesto

- 2 cups lightly packed fresh basil leaves
- 1 cup (5 oz.) firmly packed grated Parmesan cheese
- ½ to ⅔ cup olive oil
- 1 or 2 cloves garlic

In a blender or food processor, whirl basil, cheese, ½ cup of the oil, and garlic until smoothly puréed; add more oil, if necessary. If made ahead, cover and refrigerate for up to 5 days; or freeze in small, easy-to-use portions, then thaw in refrigerator overnight.

Serve over pasta, tomatoes, or hot cooked vegetables, or on toasted French bread. Makes 1½ cups.

Per tablespoon: 84 calories, 3 g protein, 1 g carbohydrate, 8 g total fat, 5 mg cholesterol, 111 mg sodium

Whipped Herb Butter

- 1 cup (½ lb.) butter or margarine, at room temperature
- 2 teaspoons lemon juice
- ⅓ cup finely chopped fresh basil, marjoram, oregano, or savory leaves; or fresh chives

In a blender or food processor, combine butter, lemon juice, and basil. Whirl until thoroughly blended. Cover and refrigerate for at least 8 hours or for up to 2 weeks; freeze for longer storage.

Serve over hot cooked vegetables or baked potatoes; use to cook omelets; or spread on hot biscuits or corn muffins. Makes about 1 cup.

Per teaspoon: 34 calories, .05 g protein, .08 g carbohydrate, 4 g total fat, 10 mg cholesterol, 39 mg sodium

Mushroom Risotto with Italian Sausage Sauce

(Pictured on page 27)

PREPARATION TIME **15** MINUTES **25** MINUTES COOKING TIME

If you'd like a pleasant change of pace from pasta, try risotto. Moist and creamy, this risotto is laced with mushrooms and crowned with a meaty tomato sauce.

- 2 tablespoons **butter** or **margarine**
- 2 tablespoons **olive oil**
- 1 small **onion,** finely chopped
- ½ pound small **mushrooms,** cut into quarters
- 1 small clove **garlic,** minced or pressed
- ⅛ teaspoon **white pepper**
- 1 cup imported **Italian rice** or **short-grain (pearl) rice**
- 2¾ cups regular-strength **chicken broth**
- ¼ cup **dry white wine**
  Italian Sausage Sauce (recipe follows)
- ½ cup **whipping cream**
- ½ cup freshly grated **Asiago** or **Parmesan cheese**
  Chopped **parsley** (optional)

In a heavy 2-quart pan, melt butter with oil over medium heat. Add onion and mushrooms; cook, stirring often, until onion is soft but not browned and liquid has evaporated. Stir in garlic, white pepper, and rice. Cook, stirring, until rice looks opaque (about 2 minutes).

Stir in broth and wine; bring mixture to a boil. Adjust heat so rice boils gently and cook, uncovered, stirring occasionally, for 15 minutes. Meanwhile, prepare Italian Sausage Sauce.

Add cream to rice mixture. Cook until rice is just tender and most of the liquid has been absorbed (about 5 more minutes; rice should still be *al dente* without tasting starchy). Stir in ¼ cup of the cheese.

Spoon rice into a warm serving bowl and top with sauce. Sprinkle with parsley, if desired. Offer remaining ¼ cup cheese to add to taste. Makes 4 servings.

Italian Sausage Sauce. Remove casings from ½ to ¾ pound **Italian sausages;** crumble meat into a 10-inch frying pan. Add 1 small **onion,** thinly sliced. Place over medium-high heat and cook, stirring, until sausage is browned. Spoon off and discard most of the drippings.

To pan add 2 medium-size **pear-shaped tomatoes,** seeded and chopped; ½ teaspoon **dry basil;** ⅛ tea-

spoon **salt;** 1 tablespoon **tomato paste;** and 1 cup **dry white wine.** Bring to a boil; reduce heat and boil gently, uncovered, stirring often, until sauce is thickened (about 10 minutes). Keep warm.

Per serving: 683 calories, 24 g protein, 51 g carbohydrates, 41 g total fat, 105 mg cholesterol, 1632 mg sodium

Wild Rice & Mushroom Pilaf with Grilled Sausages

PREPARATION TIME **8** MINUTES   **35** MINUTES COOKING TIME

With its hearty, toasted flavor and crunchy texture, wild rice pilaf deliciously complements grilled, herb-seasoned Italian sausages. Complete the menu with butter-steamed baby carrots.

- ⅔ cup **wild rice**
- 1 beef or chicken **bouillon cube**
- 2 cups **water**
- 4 fennel- or oregano-seasoned **Italian sausages** (¾ to 1 lb.)
- 3 tablespoons **butter** or **margarine**
- 1 medium-size **onion,** chopped
- ¼ pound **mushrooms,** sliced
- ⅛ teaspoon *each* **dry thyme** and **marjoram**
  Chopped **parsley**

Place wild rice in a strainer. Rinse with hot running water for about 1 minute; drain well. In a 2-quart pan, combine rice, bouillon cube, and water. Bring to a boil over high heat; reduce heat, cover, and simmer until rice is tender and has absorbed most of the water (30 to 40 minutes). Drain and discard any excess water.

Meanwhile, on a ridged cooktop grill pan or in a nonstick frying pan, grill sausages over medium heat, turning often, until sausages are browned and juices run clear when pierced (15 to 20 minutes).

While sausages are cooking, melt butter in a wide frying pan over medium heat; add onion and mushrooms and cook, stirring occasionally, until onion is soft and mushrooms are lightly browned (8 to 10 minutes).

Stir thyme and marjoram into mushroom mixture. Add rice and stir until heated through. Serve pilaf and sausages sprinkled with parsley. Makes 4 servings.

Per serving: 454 calories, 21 g protein, 24 g carbohydrates, 30 g total fat, 88 mg cholesterol, 1051 mg sodium

Eggs & Cheese

For spur-of-the-moment splendor, wrap up
an Apple & Cheese Omelet for Two (recipe on facing page).
Its golden topping is a blend of spicy, sautéed apples and sharp Cheddar cheese. To
complete a special brunch or supper, just add a basket of warm muffins.

"What's for dinner?" Fluffy scrambled eggs, a golden omelet, or a cheese-laden pizza always provide easy answers to that question. Add your own touch of elegance to these quick and popular main dishes—slivers of browned pancetta to enhance the scrambled eggs, smoked salmon or shredded Gruyère cheese to fill the omelet, a radicchio and butter lettuce salad to accompany the pizza.

Apple & Cheese Omelet for Two

(Pictured on facing page)

PREPARATION TIME   COOKING TIME

Onions sautéed with spiced apples add a savory note to this speedy entrée. Heat muffins in the oven to accompany the omelet.

2   **large tart apples**
1   **tablespoon lemon juice**
⅛   **teaspoon *each* ground nutmeg and cinnamon**
4   **tablespoons butter or margarine**
1   **small onion, finely chopped**
6   **eggs**
2   **tablespoons water**
1   **cup (4 oz.) shredded sharp Cheddar cheese**
  Apple slices and parsley sprigs (optional)

Peel, core, and slice apples into a bowl. Add lemon juice, nutmeg, and cinnamon; mix lightly.

In an 8- to 10-inch frying pan, melt 2 tablespoons of the butter over medium-high heat. Stir in apple mixture and onion. Cook, stirring often, just until apples begin to brown (6 to 8 minutes). Remove from heat and keep warm.

In a bowl, beat eggs with water until well blended. In a wide nonstick omelet pan, melt remaining 2 tablespoons butter over medium heat. Pour in eggs. Cook, gently lifting cooked portion to let uncooked egg flow underneath, until softly set. Remove from heat.

Spoon half each of the apple mixture and cheese down center of omelet. Fold a third of the omelet over filling. Slide unfolded edge onto a warm serving plate; flip folded portion over top. Spoon remaining apple mixture over omelet and sprinkle with remaining cheese. Garnish with apple slices and parsley, if desired. Makes 2 servings.

Per serving: 764 calories, 33 g protein, 27 g carbohydrates, 59 g total fat, 944 mg cholesterol, 795 mg sodium

Creamy Scrambled Eggs

PREPARATION TIME COOKING TIME

Scramble eggs with cream cheese and shallots and accompany with small, sautéed whole mushrooms. To complete the menu, offer colorful, pesto-topped baked tomato halves.

  Sautéed Mushrooms (recipe follows)
2   **tablespoons butter or margarine**
½   **cup finely chopped shallots or mild red onion**
⅓   **cup whipping cream**
1   **small package (3 oz.) cream cheese, cut into small pieces**
5   **eggs**
  Salt and pepper
  Chopped parsley (optional)

Prepare Sautéed Mushrooms; keep warm.

In an 8- to 10-inch frying pan, melt butter over low heat. Add shallots and cook, stirring, until soft (2 to 3 minutes). Add cream and cheese; stir until cheese is melted. In a bowl, lightly beat eggs; season with salt and pepper to taste.

Pour egg mixture into pan, stirring gently to blend with cream mixture. Cook just until eggs are softly set. Transfer to warm plates and sprinkle with parsley, if desired. Spoon mushrooms on top or alongside. Makes 3 or 4 servings.

Sautéed Mushrooms. In a medium-size frying pan, melt 2 tablespoons **butter** or margarine over medium-high heat. Add ½ pound small **mushrooms;** cook, stirring occasionally, until lightly browned on all sides. Season with **salt** to taste.

Per serving: 361 calories, 11 g protein, 8 g carbohydrates, 32 g total fat, 419 mg cholesterol, 278 mg sodium

To Microwave: Place butter in a 9-inch microwave-safe pie plate. Microwave on **HIGH (100%)** for 1 minute or until melted. Add shallots. Reduce whipping cream to ¼ cup and add along with cream cheese. Microwave on **HIGH (100%)** for 2 minutes; stir until smooth.

Pour in egg mixture. Microwave on **HIGH (100%)** for 2 minutes. Stir, bringing cooked portion to inside of dish, and microwave on **HIGH (100%)** for 2 more minutes. Stir again and microwave on **HIGH (100%)** for 1 more minute. Let stand for 1 minute.

Prepare and serve with mushrooms as directed.

Sprouts & Eggs

PREPARATION TIME COOKING TIME

Sprouts put fresh crunch into these eggs, scrambled with Italian sausages. Choose from mild alfalfa or the more distinctive mung or azuki bean sprouts—or use a mixture of your favorites.

- ½ **pound mild or hot Italian sausages, casings removed**
- 1 **large onion, finely chopped**
- 1 **clove garlic, minced or pressed**
- ½ **teaspoon Italian herb seasoning or dry oregano**
- ⅛ **teaspoon *each* ground nutmeg and pepper**
- 6 **eggs**
- 3 **cups alfalfa or other sprouts**
- 3 **tablespoons grated Parmesan cheese**

Crumble sausages into a wide frying pan. Cook over medium heat, stirring occasionally, until lightly browned. Add onion, garlic, Italian herb seasoning, nutmeg, and pepper. Cook, stirring often, until onion is soft (about 3 minutes).

In a bowl, beat eggs until well blended. Add to pan and cook, stirring gently, just until softly set. Stir in sprouts and sprinkle with cheese. Makes 4 servings.

Per serving: 355 calories, 20 g protein, 6 g carbohydrates, 28 g total fat, 457 mg cholesterol, 593 mg sodium

Eggs in Pepper Sauce

PREPARATION TIME   COOKING TIME

Mild mannered at breakfast, poached eggs stir up excitement for supper. Here, they join a spicy and colorful sauce of Italian sausages, sweet peppers, and green chiles.

- 1 **large red or yellow bell pepper**
- 2 **large fresh Anaheim (California) green chiles**
- 2 **tablespoons olive oil or salad oil**
- ½ **pound hot Italian sausages, cut into ½-inch-thick diagonal slices**
- 2 **cloves garlic, minced or pressed**
- 1 **large onion, thinly sliced**
- 1 **teaspoon dry basil**
- ½ **teaspoon crushed anise seeds**
- 2 **large tomatoes, coarsely chopped**
- 4 **eggs**
  Salt and pepper

Place bell pepper and chiles in a 9-inch pie pan; broil about 4 inches below heat, turning often, until charred (about 10 minutes). Cover with foil and let cool slightly. Pull off and discard skin, seeds, and stems; then thinly slice. Set aside.

Heat oil in a wide frying pan over medium heat. Add sausage slices and cook, turning occasionally, until browned. With a slotted spoon, remove sausages and set aside. To drippings add garlic, onion, basil, and anise seeds. Cook, stirring often, until onion is soft (about 3 minutes).

Return sausage to pan and add bell pepper, chiles, and tomatoes. Bring to a boil, stirring often. Reduce heat so mixture is simmering.

With a large spoon, make 4 hollows in sauce mixture, 3 to 4 inches apart. Carefully break an egg into each hollow. Cover and simmer until eggs are done to your liking (4 to 6 minutes for soft yolks). Carefully transfer each egg to a wide soup bowl or rimmed plate; spoon sauce around eggs. Season with salt and pepper to taste. Makes 4 servings.

Per serving: 391 calories, 17 g protein, 14 g carbohydrates, 31 g total fat, 317 mg cholesterol, 495 mg sodium

Avocado Huevos Rancheros

PREPARATION TIME   COOKING TIME

For an elegant variation of classic huevos rancheros, slip poached eggs into the hollows of avocado halves, then top with a bold tomato sauce. Complete a brunch or supper menu with warmed and buttered corn tortillas, hot refried beans, and—for dessert—plump strawberries to dip into powdered sugar.

- 2 **tablespoons olive oil or salad oil**
- 1 **medium-size onion, chopped**
- 1 **clove garlic, minced or pressed**
- 1 **teaspoon *each* ground cumin and dry oregano**
- 1 **large can (15 oz.) tomato sauce**
- 3 **tablespoons seeded, chopped canned green chiles**
- 1 **bay leaf**
  Salt and pepper
- 4 **or 8 Poached Eggs (directions follow)**
- 2 **avocados**
- 2 **tablespoons lemon or lime juice**
- ½ **cup shredded jack cheese**
  Shredded lettuce

Heat oil in an 8- to 10-inch frying pan over medium heat; add onion, garlic, cumin, and oregano. Cook, stirring occasionally, until onion is soft (about 5 minutes). Stir in tomato sauce, chiles, and bay leaf. Reduce heat and boil gently, uncovered, until slightly thickened (about 10 minutes). Season with salt and pepper to taste. Remove bay leaf and set sauce aside.

Prepare Poached Eggs. About 5 minutes before serving, transfer to a bowl filled with hottest tap water.

Halve, pit, and peel avocados; coat cut sides with lemon juice and place, cut sides up, in a 9-inch pie pan. Lift eggs from hot water, drain briefly, and arrange 1 or 2 eggs on each avocado half. Spoon 1 to 2 tablespoons of the sauce over top and sprinkle evenly with cheese. Broil about 6 inches below heat until cheese is melted (2 to 3 minutes).

Serve each avocado half on lettuce. Reheat remaining sauce and pass at the table. Makes 4 servings.

Poached Eggs. Fill a wide pan with enough water to cover an egg by about 1 inch. Add 1 tablespoon **vinegar** for each quart water. Bring to a simmer; reduce heat so no bubbles break surface.

Break each **egg** into water; do not crowd. Cook until set to your liking (3 to 5 minutes for soft centers). With a slotted spoon, transfer eggs to a bowl of cold water. If made ahead, cover and refrigerate for up to a day.

Per serving: 400 calories, 13 g protein, 19 g carbohydrates, 32 g total fat, 285 mg cholesterol, 918 mg sodium

To Microwave: Prepare sauce and avocados as directed. Arrange four 10-ounce microwave-safe custard cups in a circle on a flat microwave-safe plate. Pour ¼ cup water and ¼ teaspoon white vinegar into each cup. Microwave on **HIGH (100%)** for 1½ minutes or until boiling.

Carefully break an egg into each cup. With a fork, pierce membrane covering each egg yolk; then cover with plastic wrap. Microwave on **HIGH (100%)** for 2 minutes. Remove from oven and let stand for 2 minutes. Remove eggs from water and drain briefly on paper towels. Arrange an egg on each avocado half. (To offer 2 eggs per serving, poach 4 more eggs.)

Add sauce and cheese as directed. Microwave on **HIGH (100%)** for 1 minute or until cheese is melted. Serve as directed at once.

Garlic Frittata

PREPARATION TIME **30** MINUTES   **15** MINUTES BAKING TIME

An entire bulb of garlic flavors this puffy, baked frittata—but don't be alarmed. Blanching, followed by gentle sautéing, tames the pungent cloves. Serve for brunch or supper with crusty French bread and a salad of sliced tomatoes.

- 1 **small bulb garlic, separated into cloves (about ¼ cup), unpeeled**
- 3 **slices bacon**
- ½ **cup sour cream**
- 8 **eggs**
- ¼ **teaspoon salt**
- ⅛ **teaspoon *each* black pepper and ground red pepper (cayenne)**
- 3 **tablespoons grated Parmesan cheese Chopped chives**

Drop garlic into rapidly boiling water to cover. Boil, uncovered, until tender when pierced (about 5 minutes). Drain, rinse with cold water, and drain again. Remove and discard peel.

Meanwhile, in an 8½- or 9-inch ovenproof frying pan, cook bacon over medium heat until crisp (6 to 8 minutes). Lift out, drain, and chop coarsely; set aside. Reserve drippings in pan.

Add garlic to pan and cook over low heat, stirring often, until soft and lightly browned (about 5 minutes); be careful not to scorch. Remove from pan, reserving drippings, and mash garlic coarsely in a large bowl. Beat in sour cream, eggs, salt, black pepper, and red pepper until well blended.

Pour egg mixture into pan and sprinkle with bacon and cheese. Cook over medium-low heat without stirring until eggs are set at bottom (about 3 minutes).

Transfer pan to a 375° oven. Bake, uncovered, until eggs are set in center (15 to 18 minutes). Sprinkle with chives. Cut into wedges. Makes 4 servings.

Per serving: 346 calories, 17 g protein, 6 g carbohydrates, 28 g total fat, 575 mg cholesterol, 476 mg sodium

Rolled Fresh Corn Frittata

PREPARATION TIME **5** MINUTES • COOKING TIME **10** MINUTES

The difference between an omelet and a frittata is generally the amount of vegetables included—the frittata tends to offer more. This summery version is a refreshing supper for two. For a more colorful presentation, substitute red bell pepper for the green.

- **2 tablespoons butter or margarine**
- **½ to ¾ cup corn cut from cob or frozen corn kernels**
- **½ cup seeded, diced green bell pepper**
- **⅓ cup chopped green onions (including tops)**
- **4 eggs**
- **2 tablespoons whipping cream or water**
- **⅛ teaspoon liquid hot pepper seasoning Salt**

In a nonstick 9- to 10-inch frying pan, melt butter over medium-high heat. Add corn and bell pepper; cook, stirring often, until pepper is tender-crisp (about 3 minutes). Stir in onions and continue cooking until onions are soft (1 to 2 minutes); reduce heat to medium-low.

Meanwhile, beat eggs, cream, and hot pepper seasoning until well blended; season with salt to taste. Pour egg mixture over vegetables in pan. Cook, gently lifting cooked portion to let uncooked egg flow underneath, until softly set. Tilt pan and roll or fold frittata out onto a warm serving plate. Makes 2 servings.

Per serving: 363 calories, 15 g protein, 15 g carbohydrates, 28 g total fat, 596 mg cholesterol, 279 mg sodium

To Microwave: Place butter in a 9- to 10-inch microwave-safe pie plate. Microwave on **HIGH (100%)** for 2 minutes or until melted. Stir in corn, bell pepper, and onions. Microwave on **HIGH (100%)** for 3 minutes, stirring after 2 minutes.

Pour in egg mixture. Microwave on **HIGH (100%)** for 1½ minutes. Remove plate from microwave; gently lift cooked portion, tipping plate to let uncooked egg flow to edges. Microwave on **HIGH (100%)** for 2 more minutes. Let stand for 1 minute; remove from pan as directed.

Egg & Cheese Tortillas

PREPARATION TIME **9** MINUTES • COOKING TIME **8** MINUTES

Hot tortilla "sandwiches" make an easy and hearty vegetarian main dish. Or you can enliven the egg-and-cheese combination with a sprinkling of sautéed chorizo.

- **2 chorizo sausages, about 4 oz. *each* (optional), casings removed**
- **8 flour tortillas (8 inches in diameter)**
- **8 eggs**
- **2 cups (6 to 8 oz.) loosely packed shredded Cheddar cheese**
- **8 green onions, roots and tops trimmed to about 8 inches *each***
- **2 medium-size ripe tomatoes, thinly sliced**
- **1 can (4 oz.) whole green chiles, seeded and sliced into ½-inch-wide strips**

Crumble chorizo, if used, into a small frying pan. Cook over medium heat, stirring occasionally, until browned (about 5 minutes). Remove with a slotted spoon and let drain on paper towels; set aside.

For each "sandwich," place 1 tortilla in a wide frying pan over medium heat. Heat until bottom of tortilla is hot (15 to 30 seconds). Turn tortilla over and break 1 egg onto hot side. With a fork, break yolk and swirl over tortilla to within ½ inch of edge. Sprinkle with ¼ cup of the cheese and about 1½ tablespoons of the chorizo, if used. Cook, covered, until egg is set and cheese is melted (1 to 2 minutes).

Slide tortilla onto a plate. Quickly add an onion, 1 or 2 tomato slices, and a few chile strips. Roll tortilla up. Repeat with remaining tortillas, eggs, and toppings. Makes 4 servings (2 tortillas each).

Per serving: 603 calories, 33 g protein, 43 g carbohydrates, 34 g total fat, 608 mg cholesterol, 669 mg sodium

To Microwave: Crumble chorizo, if used, into an 8-inch microwave-safe dish; cover with a paper towel. Microwave on **HIGH (100%)** for 4 to 5 minutes, stirring after 2 minutes. Set aside.

For each "sandwich," place a tortilla in an 8- or 9-inch microwave-safe pie plate. Microwave on **HIGH (100%)** for 15 seconds. Break an egg onto tortilla, swirling with a fork as directed. Sprinkle with cheese and, if used, chorizo. Cover loosely with wax paper. Microwave on **HIGH (100%)** for 1 to 1½ minutes or until egg is barely set. Slide onto a serving plate; garnish and roll up as directed.

*When you want your pizza presto—and
seasoned with pizzazz—here's an appetizing version, based on
prebaked rounds of cheese-flavored bread. Individual-size Zucchini Pizza (recipe
on page 36) offers a delectable way to make use of your garden's harvest.*

Ham & Asparagus Soufflettes

PREPARATION TIME **20** MINUTES **25** MINUTES BAKING TIME

A traditional soufflé is often tedious to prepare. Our individual asparagus soufflés, by contrast, whirl together simply in a food processor or blender, then bake to puffy splendor.

> Grated Parmesan cheese
> ½ cup finely chopped cooked ham (optional)
> 1 pound asparagus, tough ends removed
> 7 eggs
> ⅓ cup whipping cream
> ½ cup shredded Swiss cheese
> 1 teaspoon Dijon mustard
> ½ teaspoon salt
> ¼ teaspoon white pepper
> ⅛ teaspoon ground nutmeg
> 8 ounces ricotta cheese
> Sour cream

Coat 4 buttered 1-cup soufflé dishes with Parmesan cheese. Sprinkle evenly with ham, if desired; place dishes on a rimmed baking sheet.

In a wide frying pan, cook asparagus in boiling water to cover over high heat just until tender when pierced (4 to 5 minutes). Drain, rinse with cold water, and pat dry with paper towels. Cut off and reserve 4 or 8 tips; cut remaining asparagus into thick slices.

In a food processor or blender, combine eggs, cream, Swiss cheese, mustard, salt, pepper, and nutmeg. Whirl until smooth. Add asparagus (all at once in processor, a third at a time in blender) and whirl until smooth. Add ricotta and whirl again until smooth.

Pour mixture evenly into prepared dishes. Bake in a 375° oven until a knife inserted in center comes out almost clean (25 to 30 minutes). Garnish with sour cream and reserved asparagus tips. Makes 4 servings.

Per serving: 343 calories, 23 g protein, 8 g carbohydrates, 24 g total fat, 532 mg cholesterol, 547 mg sodium

Chile Relleno Casserole

PREPARATION TIME **20** MINUTES **25** MINUTES BAKING TIME

While this piquant casserole bakes, cut strips of raw carrot, bell pepper, and jicama. Round out a simple, yet satisfying, supper with crusty French rolls.

> 1 large can (7 oz.) diced green chiles, drained
> 2 cups (8 oz.) shredded sharp Cheddar cheese
> 2 green onions (including tops), thinly sliced
> 2 large pear-shaped tomatoes, seeded and chopped
> 1¼ cups milk
> 4 eggs
> ½ cup all-purpose flour
> 1½ cups (6 oz.) shredded jack cheese

Spread half the chiles in a shallow 2-quart baking dish. Cover with half the Cheddar cheese, onions, and tomatoes; repeat layers, using remaining chiles, Cheddar cheese, onions, and tomatoes.

In a blender or food processor, whirl milk, eggs, and flour until smooth. Pour over mixture in baking dish. Sprinkle evenly with jack cheese.

Bake, uncovered, in a 375° oven until center jiggles only slightly when gently shaken (25 to 30 minutes). Let stand for 1 to 2 minutes; cut into squares. Makes 4 to 6 servings.

Per serving: 399 calories, 24 g protein, 16 g carbohydrates, 27 g total fat, 254 mg cholesterol, 664 mg sodium

Zucchini Pizza

(Pictured on page 35)

PREPARATION TIME **35** MINUTES **10** MINUTES BAKING TIME

Soft ricotta cheese is an unusual ingredient in pizza, but so is zucchini. Here, both join mozzarella and other delights atop puffy rounds of prebaked, cheese-sprinkled bread, available refrigerated or frozen in many supermarkets.

2 tablespoons olive oil
1 clove garlic, cut in half
½ pound medium-size zucchini (about 2), sliced ¼ inch thick
½ cup finely chopped onion
1 cup whole-milk ricotta cheese
Salt and black pepper
2 packages (8 oz. *each*) prebaked refrigerated or frozen cheese crusts (6 inches in diameter)
1 cup (about 4 oz.) slivered thinly sliced dry salami
2 cups (8 oz.) shredded mozzarella cheese
1 can (2¼ oz.) sliced ripe olives, well drained
Crushed red pepper (optional)

Heat 1 tablespoon of the oil in a wide frying pan over medium-high heat; add garlic and cook, stirring, just until golden brown. Remove and discard garlic. To oil add half the zucchini slices. Cook, turning once, until lightly browned (about 5 minutes). Drain on paper towels. To pan add remaining 1 tablespoon oil and remaining zucchini. Cook until lightly browned; then drain. Reserve drippings in pan.

Add onion; cook over medium heat, stirring often, until soft (2 to 3 minutes). Transfer to a bowl and stir in ricotta cheese; season with salt and black pepper to taste.

Place crusts in a single layer on baking sheets; spread ricotta mixture over each, almost to edge of crusts. Top with salami, zucchini, mozzarella cheese, and olives.

Bake in a 450° oven until mozzarella is melted and lightly browned (10 to 12 minutes). Season with red pepper to taste, if desired. Makes 4 servings.

Per serving: 809 calories, 36 g protein, 55 g carbohydrates, 49 g total fat, 116 mg cholesterol, 1593 mg sodium

Roasted Red Pepper Sandwiches

PREPARATION TIME **9** MINUTES   **5** MINUTES BROILING TIME

Canned roasted red peppers get these colorful open-faced sandwiches off to a quick start. For spur-of-the-moment elegance, accompany with a lemon-marinated mushroom salad and a light red wine.

4 whole wheat English muffins
8 thin slices red onion
1 large avocado

8 thin slices jack cheese (about 2½ inches square *each*)
2 jars (7 oz. *each*) roasted red bell peppers or pimentos, drained
3 tablespoons grated Parmesan cheese

Split English muffins in half and arrange, cut sides up, on a 12- by 15-inch baking sheet. Broil about 6 inches below heat until golden (about 2 minutes).

Place 1 onion slice on each muffin. Halve, pit, and peel avocado; slice each half into 8 wedges. Top each onion slice with 2 of the avocado wedges and 1 slice of the jack cheese. Add roasted peppers, dividing evenly, and sprinkle with Parmesan cheese.

Return to oven and broil until jack cheese is slightly melted (2 to 3 minutes). Makes 4 servings.

Per serving: 357 calories, 13 g protein, 39 g carbohydrates, 19 g total fat, 22 mg cholesterol, 443 mg sodium

Hearty Healthy Hotcakes

PREPARATION TIME MINUTES   MINUTES COOKING TIME

Borrow a breakfast idea for a quick dinner—fix hearty pancakes of mixed grains. Serve with fresh fruit, a slice of ham perhaps, and your favorite syrup.

⅓ cup *each* regular rolled oats, cornmeal, and all-purpose flour
2 tablespoons sugar
1 teaspoon baking powder
½ teaspoon baking soda
¼ teaspoon salt
2 eggs, separated
1 cup buttermilk
Salad oil

Combine oats, cornmeal, flour, sugar, baking powder, baking soda, and salt. In another bowl, whisk egg yolks and buttermilk until blended. Pour liquid into dry ingredients, stirring just until evenly moistened.

With an electric mixer, beat egg whites at high speed until soft peaks form. Gently fold whites into batter.

Heat an electric griddle to 375° (or heat a wide frying pan or griddle over medium-high heat until a drop of water sizzles on it). Brush lightly with oil. For each pancake, spoon about ⅓ cup of the batter onto griddle. Cook until top is set and bottom is browned (about 1 minute). Turn and cook until other side is browned (about 30 seconds). Makes about 8 pancakes.

Per pancake: 117 calories, 4 g protein, 15 g carbohydrates, 4 g total fat, 70 mg cholesterol, 222 mg sodium

Fish & Shellfish

*It's hard to believe that it only takes about 15 minutes
to prepare and bake Sole with Pistachio Butter Sauce (recipe on facing page).
To accompany such a culinary triumph, choose simple side dishes—
a tossed salad and hot, crusty rolls.*

When time is short, seafood suggests an entrée that's both elegant and effortless. Whether you sauté, bake, broil, or grill, the interval from refrigerator to table is bound to be brief. In fact, you'll have to take care not to overcook fish and shellfish (it helps to have all ingredients ready before you start). With the recipes in this chapter, you can sit down to your trout, scallops, or other favorite seafood, after only a few minutes spent in the kitchen.

Snapper Florentine

PREPARATION TIME   BAKING TIME

Cloaked with a tart and creamy sauce, thick fish fillets bake briefly, then arrive at the table atop a bed of spinach. This dish can also be prepared conveniently in a microwave oven.

- ¾ **cup sour cream**
- ⅓ **cup mayonnaise**
- 2 **tablespoons** *each* **all-purpose flour and lemon juice**
- ¼ **teaspoon dill weed**
- 1 **pound red snapper fillets (about ½ inch thick)**
  Salt and pepper
- 2 **bunches spinach (1½ to 2 lbs.** *total***), rinsed and stemmed**
  Paprika

Combine sour cream, mayonnaise, flour, lemon juice, and dill weed. Stir with a wire whisk until smoothly blended; set aside.

Rinse fish and pat dry. Arrange in a single layer in a 9- by 13-inch baking dish. Season with salt and pepper to taste. Spread sour cream mixture over fish. Bake, uncovered, in a 400° oven until fish flakes when prodded in thickest part with a fork (about 10 minutes).

Meanwhile, place spinach (with water that clings to leaves) in a wide frying pan over medium-high heat. Cover and cook, stirring occasionally, until wilted and bright green in color (2 to 4 minutes); drain well.

Arrange spinach on a warm platter. Place fish on top. Spoon any sauce remaining in baking dish over fish; sprinkle with paprika. Makes 4 servings.

Per serving: 380 calories, 29 g protein, 12 g carbohydrates, 25 g total fat, 92 mg cholesterol, 333 mg sodium

To Microwave: Prepare sour cream mixture as directed. Place spinach in a 3-quart microwave-safe casserole. Microwave, covered, on **HIGH (100%)** for 4 to 5 minutes, stirring once. Let stand, covered.

Rinse fish and pat dry. Place in a 7- by 11-inch or 10-inch round microwave-safe dish, with thickest portions toward outside of dish; season with salt and pepper to taste. Microwave, uncovered, on **HIGH (100%)** for 3 minutes. Rotate each fillet a half-turn and spread with sour cream mixture. Microwave on **HIGH (100%)** for 3 minutes; then let stand for 3 minutes.

Meanwhile, drain spinach and arrange on a warm platter. Top with fish, sauce, and paprika as directed.

Sole with Pistachio Butter Sauce

(Pictured on facing page)

PREPARATION TIME 10 COOKING TIME

Swirled in a butter-vermouth sauce, pistachios add a touch of elegance to sautéed sole. To balance a memorable entrée, serve with a green salad.

- 1½ **pounds sole fillets**
  All-purpose flour
  About ⅓ cup butter or margarine
  About 2 tablespoons salad oil
- ¼ **cup thinly sliced green onions (including tops)**
- ½ **cup** *each* **dry vermouth and regular-strength chicken broth**
- ⅓ **cup roasted salted or unsalted shelled pistachios, coarsely chopped (about ⅔ cup nuts in the shell)**
  Lemon wedges
  Italian parsley

Rinse fish and pat dry; dust with flour, shaking off excess. In a wide frying pan, melt 1 tablespoon of the butter with 1 tablespoon of the oil over medium-high heat. Add fillets; do not crowd. Cook, turning once, until fish flakes when prodded in thickest part with a fork (about 2 minutes total). Lift out and place on a warm platter; keep warm. Repeat until all fish is cooked, adding butter and oil as needed.

To pan add onions, vermouth, and broth; boil, uncovered, over high heat until reduced by half. Reduce heat to low and add ¼ cup butter; stir constantly until butter is completely blended into sauce. Stir in pistachios; then spoon sauce over fish. Garnish with lemon and parsley. Makes 4 or 5 servings.

Per serving: 336 calories, 24 g protein, 7 g carbohydrates, 23 g total fat, 97 mg cholesterol, 435 mg sodium

Macadamia Parmesan Sole

PREPARATION TIME **10** MINUTES   **10** MINUTES BAKING TIME

Chopped macadamia nuts add crunch to delicate sole fillets. Alongside, offer fresh asparagus or broccoli spears and lemony rice.

- 2 **eggs**
- ¾ **cup freshly grated Parmesan cheese**
- 2 **tablespoons all-purpose flour**
- 4 **sole fillets (4 to 6 oz. *each*)**
- 3 **tablespoons salad oil**
- 3 **tablespoons butter or margarine**
- ½ **cup finely chopped roasted salted macadamia nuts**
  Watercress or parsley sprigs
  Lemon halves

Place a 10- by 15-inch rimmed baking pan in oven as it preheats to 425°.

In a shallow pan, beat eggs until blended. On wax paper, combine cheese and flour. Rinse fish and pat dry. Dip each fillet in egg to coat; drain briefly. Then coat with cheese mixture. Place fish in a single layer on wax paper.

Remove pan from oven; add oil and butter and swirl until butter is melted. Lay a fillet in pan, turning to coat with butter-oil mixture. Repeat with remaining fillets, arranging pieces slightly apart in pan. Sprinkle with nuts.

Bake, uncovered, in a 425° oven until fish flakes when prodded in thickest part with a fork (7 to 10 minutes). Transfer fish to a warm platter. Garnish with watercress and lemon. Makes 4 servings.

Per serving: 538 calories, 39 g protein, 6 g carbohydrates, 40 g total fat, 253 mg cholesterol, 651 mg sodium

Sole with Garlic Sauce

PREPARATION TIME **7** MINUTES   **30** MINUTES COOKING TIME

Slow cooking in butter tames an impressive quantity of garlic to sweet pungency—a perfect seasoning for sole fillets. Serve a green pasta as an accompaniment to share the marvelous sauce.

About ⅓ **cup butter or margarine**
- ¼ **cup finely chopped garlic (about 12 large cloves)**
- 1 **pound sole fillets**
  Salt and pepper
- 1 **egg**
- 1 **tablespoon water**
  About 2 tablespoons salad oil
  Lemon wedges

In a small frying pan, melt 3 tablespoons of the butter over medium-low heat. Add garlic and cook, stirring occasionally, until garlic just begins to turn golden (about 15 minutes). Remove from heat and keep warm.

Rinse fish and pat dry. Season with salt and pepper to taste. In a shallow pan, lightly beat egg and water. In a wide frying pan, heat 1 tablespoon *each* of the butter and salad oil over medium heat until frothy. Dip each fillet in egg mixture to coat; drain briefly. Arrange in pan; do not crowd.

Cook, turning once, until fish flakes when prodded in thickest part with a fork (about 2 minutes total). Lift out and place on a warm platter; keep warm. Repeat until all fish is cooked, adding more butter and oil as needed.

Pour garlic sauce over fish and garnish with lemon. Makes 3 or 4 servings.

Per serving: 317 calories, 21 g protein, 3 g carbohydrates, 24 g total fat, 163 mg cholesterol, 293 mg sodium

Monkfish Scaloppine with Olives

PREPARATION TIME **15** MINUTES   **15** MINUTES COOKING TIME

Known for its delicate flavor and lobsterlike texture, monkfish takes well to slicing, pounding, sautéing, and saucing in this version of scaloppine. Serve with buttered fresh pasta and a green salad.

- 1 **large monkfish fillet (1 to 1½ lbs.)**
  All-purpose flour
  About 2 tablespoons butter or margarine
  About 2 tablespoons salad oil
- 2 **tablespoons olive oil**
- 1 **small red bell pepper, seeded and diced**
- 3 **cloves garlic, minced or pressed**
- 1 **can (6 oz.) pitted black ripe olives, drained**
- ¼ **cup chopped parsley**
- ⅔ **cup regular-strength chicken broth**
- 2 **tablespoons lemon juice**

Rinse fish and pat dry. If fillet is encased in a tough membrane, cut it off from one side of fillet. Then lay fillet on a board, membrane side down. Starting 3 to 4 inches from tapered end of fillet, cut toward tapered end at about a 45° angle to form a ¼- to ⅜-inch-thick slice. At base of fillet, angle knife to slice flesh free of membrane on bottom. Continue slicing fillet until pieces become too short for large slices. Cut membrane from remaining triangular chunk. Then cut almost through thickest part of chunk; open to flatten.

Place fish slices between sheets of plastic wrap. With a flat-surfaced mallet, gently pound fish until slices are about ⅛ inch thick. Coat fish with flour, shaking off excess, and place in a single layer on wax paper.

In a wide frying pan, melt 1 tablespoon of the butter with 1 tablespoon of the salad oil over medium-high heat. Add fish; do not crowd. Cook, turning once, until fish flakes when prodded in center with a fork (1½ to 2 minutes total). Lift out and place on a warm platter; keep warm. Repeat until all fish is cooked, adding more butter and oil as needed.

In same pan, combine olive oil, bell pepper, and garlic. Cook over medium heat, stirring often, until pepper is limp. Add olives, parsley, broth, and lemon juice. Boil, uncovered, over high heat until liquid is reduced by half. Spoon sauce over fish. Makes 4 servings.

Per serving: 414 calories, 28 g protein, 7 g carbohydrates, 31 g total fat, 75 mg cholesterol, 856 mg sodium

Oven-fried Orange Roughy with Sesame Seeds

PREPARATION TIME **5** MINUTES   **13** MINUTES BAKING TIME

Orange roughy, caught in the South Pacific, is a newcomer to our shores. Moist, firm, and white fleshed, it takes well to baking quickly in a hot oven, a method that doesn't require turning the fish. Serve with steamed rice and fresh peas.

 1 **egg white**
 ⅓ **cup sesame seeds**
 4 **boned, skinned orange roughy (New Zealand perch) fillets (6 to 8 oz. *each*), thawed if frozen**
 2 **tablespoons salad oil**
    Lemon wedges
    Soy sauce

In a shallow pan, beat egg white until slightly frothy. Spread sesame seeds in another shallow pan.

Rinse fish and pat dry. Dip fillets on one side only in egg white; drain briefly. Then generously coat egg-moistened side with sesame seeds. Place fillets, seed sides up, in a single layer on wax paper.

Place a 10- by 15-inch rimmed baking pan in a 500° oven and heat for about 5 minutes. Swirl oil in pan; then lay fillets, seed sides down, in pan. Bake, uncovered, on lowest oven rack until fish flakes when prodded in thickest part with a fork and seeds are lightly browned (about 8 minutes). Arrange each fillet, seed side up, on a dinner plate. Offer lemon and soy to add to taste. Makes 4 servings.

Per serving: 400 calories, 47 g protein, 3 g carbohydrates, 22 g total fat, 125 mg cholesterol, 127 mg sodium

Testing Fish for Doneness

Recognizing when fish is done is essential to cooking it well. Most recipes tell you to cook fish until it "flakes when prodded." At this point, the tender flesh slides apart along its natural divisions at the gentle probing of a fork. Another moment or two of cooking and flavor and moisture begin to escape.

Test at the center of the thickest portion of the whole fish, steak, or fillet—thinner parts may appear to be done while thicker portions are still cool and uncooked inside.

A rule of thumb for estimating cooking time for fish cooked by any method other than microwaving is to allow 8 to 10 minutes for each inch of thickness.

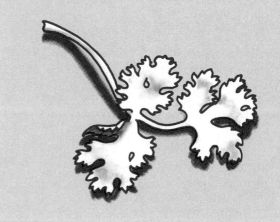

Broiled Fish Dijon

PREPARATION TIME **5** MINUTES   **12** MINUTES BROILING TIME

Exuberant seasonings enliven firm-fleshed fish fillets in this quick and easy entrée. Serve it either hot or cold, accompanied with stir-fried green and yellow summer squash.

- 4 **firm-textured white fish fillets, such as sea bass or rockfish, ¾ to 1 inch thick (6 to 8 oz. *each*)**
- 4 **teaspoons lemon juice**
- 3 **tablespoons Dijon mustard**
- 1 **clove garlic, minced or pressed**
- ⅛ **teaspoon paprika**
- 2 **tablespoons drained capers**

Rinse fish and pat dry. Arrange in a single layer in a 10- by 15-inch rimmed baking pan or broiler pan. Drizzle lemon juice over fillets.

In a small bowl, stir together mustard and garlic; spread over top of each fillet.

Broil 6 to 8 inches below heat until fish flakes when prodded in thickest part with a fork (10 to 14 minutes); rotate pan if necessary to cook fish evenly.

Sprinkle fillets with paprika and capers. Transfer to a warm platter and serve hot. Or, to serve cold, let fish cool; then cover and refrigerate for at least 30 minutes or up to 2 hours. Makes 4 servings.

Per serving: 227 calories, 44 g protein, 2 g carbohydrates, 3 g total fat, 125 mg cholesterol, 599 mg sodium

Broiled Swordfish with Tomato-Olive Confetti

(Pictured on facing page)

PREPARATION TIME **15** MINUTES   **11** MINUTES BROILING TIME

To give its flavors time to blend, make the colorful vegetable sauce first. Then, to serve with the swordfish, bake tiny new potatoes. Keep them warm as you prepare the brightly sauced swordfish steaks.

- **Tomato-Olive Confetti (recipe follows)**
- 1½ **pounds swordfish steaks (about 1 inch thick)**
- 1 **tablespoon olive oil or salad oil**
- 3 **cups lightly packed watercress sprigs, washed and crisped**
- **Lime wedges (optional)**

Prepare Tomato-Olive Confetti and set aside.

Cut fish into 4 equal portions; rinse and pat dry. Place on an oiled rack in a 12- by 14-inch broiler pan. Brush top of fish with oil. Broil about 5 inches below heat for 5 minutes. Turn fish over, brush with oil, and broil until fish flakes when prodded in thickest part with a fork (5 to 6 more minutes).

Arrange watercress on 4 dinner plates and lay fish on top. Spoon Tomato-Olive Confetti over fish. Garnish with lime, if desired. Makes 4 servings.

Tomato-Olive Confetti. Stir together 1 medium-size **tomato,** seeded and finely chopped; ½ cup sliced **pimento-stuffed green olives;** 2 tablespoons drained **capers;** and 3 tablespoons *each* sliced **green onions** (including tops), **lime juice,** and **olive oil** or salad oil.

Per serving: 347 calories, 33 g protein, 3 g carbohydrates, 22 g total fat, 91 mg cholesterol, 624 mg sodium

Cheese-topped Baked Halibut

PREPARATION TIME **8** MINUTES   **15** MINUTES BAKING TIME

A coating of mayonnaise and sour cream preserves the moist succulence of halibut steaks as they bake. To enjoy with the fish, bake crumb-topped tomato halves in the same oven.

- 2 **pounds halibut steaks (about 1 inch thick)**
- ½ **cup *each* mayonnaise and sour cream**
- 2 **teaspoons all-purpose flour**
- 1½ **teaspoons lemon juice**
- 1 **tablespoon minced onion**
- ⅛ **teaspoon ground red pepper (cayenne)**
- ½ **cup shredded Cheddar cheese**

Rinse halibut steaks and pat dry. Arrange in a greased 8- by 12-inch baking pan.

In a small bowl, mix mayonnaise, sour cream, and flour until smooth; stir in lemon juice, onion, and red pepper. Spoon mixture evenly over fish, covering completely.

Bake, uncovered, in a 425° oven until fish flakes when prodded in center with a fork (12 to 14 minutes). Sprinkle with cheese and continue to bake just until cheese is melted (about 2 more minutes). Makes 4 to 6 servings.

Per serving: 337 calories, 29 g protein, 2 g carbohydrates, 23 g total fat, 90 mg cholesterol, 239 mg sodium

Its festive salsa topping boldly announces
Broiled Swordfish with Tomato-Olive Confetti (recipe on facing page),
served here on a bed of equally spirited watercress. Moist and meaty,
swordfish is a natural vehicle for flavorful accents.

*Can a hurry-up entrée present an
elegant dining experience? If you're skeptical, try
Scallops & Shrimp in Béarnaise Cream (recipe on facing page), adorned with a
tarragon sprig and accompanied with fresh broccoli. There's your answer.*

46

Scallops & Shrimp in Béarnaise Cream

(Pictured on facing page)

PREPARATION TIME COOKING TIME

The moist, tender textures and delicate flavors of scallops and shrimp blend in this tarragon-seasoned cream sauce. Steam spears of broccoli or asparagus to complement the seafood.

- **2 tablespoons butter or margarine**
- **1 pound sea scallops, rinsed and cut in half horizontally**
- **½ pound large raw shrimp, peeled and deveined**
- **⅓ cup finely chopped shallots**
- **¾ cup tarragon wine vinegar or white wine vinegar**
- **½ cup regular-strength chicken broth**
- **¼ teaspoon dry tarragon**
- **1 tablespoon Dijon mustard**
- **½ cup whipping cream**
  Salt and white pepper
  Fresh tarragon sprigs (optional)

In a wide frying pan, melt butter over medium-high heat. Add scallops and shrimp; cook, stirring, just until seafood is opaque in thickest part when cut (3 to 4 minutes). With a slotted spoon, transfer seafood to a bowl and set aside. Reserve drippings in pan.

Add shallots, vinegar, broth, and dry tarragon to pan. Boil, uncovered, over high heat until liquid is reduced to ½ cup. Pour any accumulated juices from seafood into pan along with mustard and cream. Bring again to a boil and cook until sauce is reduced to about ¾ cup. Stir in seafood. Season with salt and white pepper to taste. Garnish each serving with fresh tarragon, if desired. Makes 4 servings.

Per serving: 315 calories, 31 g protein, 9 g carbohydrates, 17 g total fat, 156 mg cholesterol, 588 mg sodium

To Microwave: Combine butter, scallops, and shrimp in a 3-quart microwave-safe casserole. Microwave, covered, on **HIGH (100%)** for 6 minutes, stirring once; let stand for 2 minutes. Using a slotted spoon, transfer seafood to a bowl, cover, and set aside.

Add remaining ingredients except salt and white pepper to casserole, reducing vinegar to ½ cup and omitting chicken broth. Microwave, uncovered, on

HIGH (100%) for 10 to 12 minutes or until liquid is reduced to about ¾ cup. Stir in seafood and season with salt and white pepper to taste.

Scallops & Tomato au Gratin

PREPARATION TIME   COOKING TIME

Around each serving of scallops, spoon steamed rice to profit from the exquisite seafood sauce. Complete the repast with a crisp spinach salad.

- **1½ pounds sea scallops**
- **2 tablespoons butter or margarine**
- **1 tablespoon salad oil**
- **¼ cup thinly sliced shallots**
- **6 mushrooms, sliced**
- **1 small pear-shaped tomato, seeded and chopped**
- **1 teaspoon minced fresh tarragon leaves or ¼ teaspoon dry tarragon**
- **¼ teaspoon salt**
- **⅓ cup dry white wine**
- **½ cup whipping cream**
- **½ cup shredded Gruyère or Swiss cheese**

Rinse scallops and pat dry. In a wide frying pan, melt butter with oil over medium-high heat. Add scallops; cook, stirring gently, just until scallops are opaque in center when cut (about 2 minutes). With a slotted spoon, transfer scallops to a bowl and set aside; reserve drippings in pan.

Add shallots and mushrooms to pan; cook over high heat, stirring often, just until mushrooms are lightly browned and most of the liquid has evaporated. Stir in tomato, tarragon, salt, and wine. Boil, stirring occasionally, until most of the liquid has evaporated. Add cream; boil, stirring often, until liquid is reduced by about half and large, shiny bubbles appear.

Pour any accumulated juices from scallops into pan; bring to a boil and cook until sauce has thickened. Remove from heat and lightly mix in scallops.

Spoon mixture into four 7-inch scallop shells or shallow individual baking dishes. Place on a rimmed baking sheet. Sprinkle with cheese. Broil about 4 inches below heat until cheese is melted and tops are lightly browned (2 to 3 minutes). Makes 4 servings.

Per serving: 403 calories, 35 g protein, 10 g carbohydrates, 25 g total fat, 127 mg cholesterol, 531 mg sodium

Broiled Oysters, Bacon & Cheese

PREPARATION TIME **20** MINUTES **8** MINUTES BROILING TIME

Tender oysters nestle under a savory blanket of bell pepper and onion strips, melted cheese, and crisp bacon. Round out a superb—yet simple—supper with hot buttered toast and iced tea or beer.

- 6 slices bacon
- 1 medium-size green bell pepper, seeded and cut into julienne strips
- 1 small onion, thinly slivered
- 2 jars (10 oz. *each*) small Pacific oysters, drained and patted dry
- ¾ cup shredded Cheddar cheese
  Hot buttered French bread toast (optional)

In a wide frying pan, cook bacon over medium heat until crisp. Lift out, drain, and crumble; set aside. Discard all but 1½ tablespoons of the drippings.

Add bell pepper and onion to pan. Cook, stirring occasionally, until onion is soft (4 to 6 minutes).

Meanwhile, arrange oysters in a single layer in a heatproof 9- by 12-inch pan or shallow 2-quart serving dish. Broil about 3 inches below heat just until edges of oysters begin to curl (about 3 minutes); turn and broil until edges curl again (about 3 more minutes).

Spoon onion mixture over oysters and sprinkle with cheese and bacon. Broil just until cheese is melted (1 to 2 minutes). Garnish with toast, if desired. Makes 4 servings.

Per serving: 280 calories, 18 g protein, 8 g carbohydrates, 19 g total fat, 140 mg cholesterol, 412 mg sodium

Crab Lace Patties on Lettuce

PREPARATION TIME **15** MINUTES **6** MINUTES COOKING TIME

In a medley of delicious contrasts, hot, crispy crab cakes combine with cool, delicate avocado and lettuce. For heartiness, add warm corn bread or toasted English muffins.

- ¾ pound crabmeat
- ¾ cup grated Parmesan cheese
- 2 tablespoons minced parsley
- ½ teaspoon dry oregano
- 2 cloves garlic, minced or pressed
- ¼ cup fine dry bread crumbs
- 2 green onions (including tops), thinly sliced
- 1 egg, beaten
- ¼ cup whipping cream
  About 1 tablespoon olive oil or salad oil
- 1 large avocado
- 8 to 12 large butter lettuce leaves, washed and crisped

Break crab into flakes. Add cheese, parsley, oregano, garlic, bread crumbs, onions, egg, and cream; mix lightly.

Heat 2 teaspoons of the oil in a wide frying pan over medium heat. For each patty, mound 3 tablespoons of the crab mixture in pan, spreading to make a 3-inch cake. Cook until bottom is lightly browned (about 2 minutes). Turn and cook until other side is very lightly browned (about 1 minute); keep warm. Repeat until all patties are cooked, adding more oil as needed.

Pit, peel, and slice avocado. On 4 dinner plates, arrange lettuce, avocado slices, and crab patties. Makes 4 servings.

Per serving: 374 calories, 25 g protein, 12 g carbohydrates, 25 g total fat, 182 mg cholesterol, 535 mg sodium

Cracked Crab with Red Pepper Aïoli

PREPARATION TIME **15** MINUTES **15** MINUTES COOKING TIME

Cold cracked crab turns festive when dipped in a tangy mayonnaise made with broiled red bell peppers. To share the aïoli, offer artichokes (or other blanched or crisp fresh vegetables) and sourdough bread alongside.

2 red bell peppers
1 tablespoon olive oil
½ teaspoon dry thyme
1 or 2 cloves garlic, slivered
¼ teaspoon salt
1 tablespoon white wine vinegar
1 egg
½ cup *each* salad oil and olive oil
2 or 3 cooked Dungeness crabs in the shell (1½ to 2 lbs. *each*), cleaned and cracked

Brush bell peppers with the 1 tablespoon olive oil and sprinkle with thyme. Place on a rack in a broiler pan. Broil about 4 inches below heat, turning often, until peppers are dappled with brown spots (10 to 15 minutes). Let cool slightly; cut into quarters, removing stems and seeds.

In a blender or food processor, whirl bell peppers, garlic, salt, vinegar, and egg until smooth. With motor running, add salad oil and the ½ cup olive oil in a thin, steady stream. If made ahead, cover and refrigerate aïoli for up to a week.

Rinse crab under cold running water to remove loose bits of shell. Pat dry with paper towels. Pile crab onto a platter. As you shell crab to eat, dip meat into aïoli. Makes 4 to 6 servings.

Per serving of crab: 25 calories, 5 g protein, .13 g carbohydrate, .51 g total fat, 27 mg cholesterol, 57 mg sodium

Per tablespoon of aïoli: 68 calories, .22 g protein, .33 g carbohydrate, 7 g total fat, 9 mg cholesterol, 19 mg sodium

Sautéed Hoisin Shrimp

PREPARATION TIME MINUTES   COOKING TIME MINUTES

To balance these gloriously spicy stir-fried shrimp, serve slivered bok choy (Chinese chard cabbage), also from your wok. Distinctive soybean-based hoisin sauce is a favorite with Chinese cooks.

3 tablespoons hoisin sauce
2 tablespoons *each* vinegar and water
2 teaspoons sugar
½ teaspoon *each* ground ginger and cornstarch
⅛ teaspoon crushed red pepper
2 tablespoons salad oil
1 pound medium-size raw shrimp (30 to 32 per lb.), shelled and deveined
1 clove garlic, minced or pressed
6 green onions (including tops), diagonally cut into 1-inch lengths

Mix hoisin sauce, vinegar, water, sugar, ginger, cornstarch, and red pepper; set aside.

Heat oil in a wide frying pan or wok over medium-high heat. Add shrimp and garlic and cook, stirring occasionally, for about 2 minutes. Add onions and hoisin mixture and cook, stirring, until sauce is thickened and shrimp are opaque in thickest part when cut (about 3 minutes). Makes 4 servings.

Per serving: 190 calories, 20 g protein, 8 g carbohydrates, 8 g total fat, 131 mg cholesterol, 575 mg sodium

Sautéed Shrimp in Mint Beurre Blanc

PREPARATION TIME MINUTES   COOKING TIME MINUTES

Cool, fresh mint brightens the rich butter sauce that bathes these quickly cooked shrimp. Serve sliced tomatoes alongside, as well as tiny new potatoes steamed in their jackets.

6 or 8 tablespoons butter or margarine
½ teaspoon grated lemon peel
1 cup packed mint leaves
1 to 1½ pounds medium-size raw shrimp (30 to 32 per lb.), shelled and deveined
1 cup dry white wine
Lemon slices
Fresh mint sprigs

In a food processor or blender, whirl 4 tablespoons of the butter, lemon peel, and mint leaves until well blended; set aside.

In a wide frying pan, melt 2 more tablespoons of the butter over medium heat. Add shrimp and cook, stirring, until shrimp turn pink (about 5 minutes). With a slotted spoon, lift out shrimp; keep warm. Reserve drippings in pan.

Add wine to pan and boil over high heat, stirring often, until liquid is reduced to ⅓ cup (about 5 minutes). Add mint butter all in one chunk; stir quickly until butter is completely blended into sauce. (For a thicker sauce, stir in 2 more tablespoons butter.) Pour sauce into a warm serving dish; then add shrimp. Garnish with lemon and mint sprigs. Makes 4 servings.

Per serving: 308 calories, 29 g protein, 3 g carbohydrates, 19 g total fat, 243 mg cholesterol, 467 mg sodium

Malaysian Hot Shrimp

PREPARATION TIME 30 MINUTES   10 MINUTES COOKING TIME

Hot chiles lend strong seasoning to this Southeast Asian shrimp dish. To soothe the chiles' fire, serve steamed rice. Start cooking the rice while the chiles are softening.

- **3 small dried hot red chiles, seeded**
- **1½ tablespoons tamarind paste; or 1½ tablespoons cider vinegar and ¼ teaspoon sugar**
- **1 teaspoon shrimp paste or sauce (*blachan*); or anchovy paste**
- **¼ cup tomato paste**
- **2 tablespoons salad oil**
- **2 tablespoons minced shallots**
- **2 cloves garlic, minced or pressed**
- **1 small onion, thinly sliced**
- **1 pound jumbo raw shrimp (16 to 20 per lb.), shelled and deveined**
- **Fresh cilantro (coriander) sprigs**

Cover chiles with hot water and let stand until soft (about 10 minutes). In a small bowl, combine tamarind paste and ¼ cup water; with your hands, separate seeds from paste. (Or mix vinegar and sugar with 3 tablespoons water.)

Press tamarind mixture through a wire strainer into a blender or food processor; discard solids remaining in strainer. (Or pour vinegar mixture into blender.) Drain chiles and add to blender with shrimp paste, tomato paste, and 2 tablespoons water; whirl until puréed. Set aside.

Heat oil in a wide frying pan or wok over medium-high heat. Add shallots, garlic, and onion; cook, stirring, until onion is soft (2 to 3 minutes). Stir in tamarind mixture and cook, stirring, until mixture boils.

Reduce heat to medium and add shrimp; cook, stirring often, just until shrimp are opaque in thickest part when cut (4 to 5 minutes). Garnish with cilantro. Makes 3 or 4 servings.

Per serving: 196 calories, 21 g protein, 8 g carbohydrates, 9 g total fat, 131 mg cholesterol, 336 mg sodium

To Microwave: Prepare chiles, tamarind paste, and blender mixture as directed.

In a 9- to 10-inch round microwave-safe dish, combine oil, shallots, garlic, and onion; microwave, uncovered, on **HIGH (100%)** for 3 to 4 minutes or until shallots are soft. Stir in tamarind mixture. Microwave on **HIGH (100%)** for 4 to 5 minutes or until onion is very soft.

Stir shrimp into sauce and microwave on **HIGH (100%)** for 3 minutes, stirring every minute to bring shrimp to center of dish. Cover with plastic wrap and let stand for 3 minutes. Shrimp should be opaque when cut in center. If not done, cover and microwave on **HIGH (100%)** until opaque, checking every 30 seconds. Garnish with cilantro.

Broiled Prawns Wrapped in Bacon

(Pictured on facing page)

PREPARATION TIME 30 MINUTES   8 MINUTES BROILING TIME

Jumbo shrimp—also called prawns—make a handsome and flavorful entrée when wrapped in bacon, skewered, and broiled.

- **8 slices bacon**
- **16 jumbo raw shrimp (16 to 20 per lb.)**

In a wide frying pan, cook bacon over medium heat until some of the fat has cooked out and bacon begins to brown (3 to 4 minutes); bacon should not be crisp. Drain, then cut each slice in half lengthwise.

Shell (except for tails) and devein shrimp. Wrap a bacon strip around each shrimp. Thread shrimp, as shown in photo on facing page, on 10-inch-long bamboo skewers.

Place on a rack in a broiler pan and broil about 4 inches below heat, turning once, until bacon is golden brown and prawns are opaque in thickest part when cut (6 to 10 minutes total). Makes 4 servings.

Per serving: 168 calories, 23 g protein, .07 g carbohydrate, 8 g total fat, 141 mg cholesterol, 394 mg sodium

To Microwave: Place bacon on several thicknesses of paper towels; cover with another paper towel. Microwave on **HIGH (100%)** for 5 minutes or until bacon is lightly browned but not crisp.

Wrap shrimp in bacon and skewer as directed. Arrange on a microwave-safe roasting rack or several thicknesses of fresh paper towels. Cover with a paper towel. Microwave on **HIGH (100%)** for 4 to 6 minutes, reversing direction of skewers once, until bacon is browned and shrimp are opaque in thickest part when cut.

*A skewered feast, Broiled Prawns Wrapped
in Bacon (recipe on facing page) spearheads a summer menu
that's as easy and delicious as the season itself. As accents, offer fresh
fruit and a rice pilaf.*

Quick Accompaniments

Many popular quick entrées—grilled steaks, broiled fish, and baked chicken, for example—are so simple that they leave plenty of room for imagination in choosing dishes to accompany them. Certain seasonal vegetables, such as steamed asparagus or field-fresh ears of corn, are stylish enough to stand on their own. But even the last-minute chef can whip up more unconventional side dishes, such as the ones below.

Cheddar Cheese Potato Salad

½ cup chopped bacon
1 medium-size onion, chopped
1 pound thin-skinned potatoes, boiled and cut into ½-inch cubes
4 hard-cooked eggs, chopped
½ cup Cheddar cheese cubes (about ¼ inch square)
½ cup mayonnaise
2 teaspoons prepared mustard
Salt and pepper

In a wide frying pan, cook bacon over medium heat, stirring occasionally, until crisp. Remove with a slotted spoon and transfer to a large bowl; reserve drippings in pan.

Add onion to pan and cook, stirring often, until soft. Remove with a slotted spoon and add to bacon, along with potatoes, eggs, cheese, mayonnaise, and mustard; mix lightly. Season with salt and pepper to taste. If made ahead, cover and refrigerate for up to a day. Makes 6 servings.

Per serving: 385 calories, 10 g protein, 17 g carbohydrates, 31 g total fat, 214 mg cholesterol, 348 mg sodium

Roasted Onion Halves

3 large onions (3 to 3½ inches in diameter)
¼ cup balsamic or red wine vinegar (optional)
Butter or margarine
Salt and pepper

Cut onions in half lengthwise. If desired, pour vinegar into a 9- by 13-inch baking pan. Place onions, cut sides down, in pan.

Bake, uncovered, in a 350° oven until onions are soft when pressed (30 to 45 minutes). Pass butter and salt and pepper to add to taste. Makes 3 to 6 servings.

Per serving: 29 calories, .94 g protein, 6 g carbohydrates, .20 g total fat, 0 mg cholesterol, 2 mg sodium

Almond Pilaf with Sherry

(Pictured on page 94)

½ cup slivered blanched almonds
½ cup dry vermicelli, broken into 1-inch lengths
¼ cup butter or margarine
1 cup long-grain white rice
1¼ cups regular-strength chicken broth
¾ cup cream sherry
1½ teaspoons dry tarragon or 1 tablespoon chopped fresh tarragon leaves
Fresh tarragon sprigs (optional)

In a wide frying pan, stir almonds over medium-high heat until golden brown (about 4 minutes); remove from pan and set aside. Add vermicelli to pan and stir until golden brown (about 2 minutes); remove from pan and set aside.

Add butter and rice to pan; stir until rice is lightly toasted (about 3 minutes). Add broth, sherry, dry tarragon, and vermicelli. Bring mixture to a boil; reduce heat, cover, and simmer until rice is tender to bite (20 to 25 minutes). Sprinkle with toasted almonds and garnish with fresh tarragon. Makes 5 or 6 servings.

Per serving: 354 calories, 6 g protein, 34 g carbohydrates, 21 g total fat, 41 mg cholesterol, 370 mg sodium

Sautéed Red Peppers with Basil

2 large red bell peppers, seeded
2 tablespoons salad oil
2 tablespoons chopped fresh basil leaves or 1 teaspoon dry basil
Salt and pepper
Fresh basil sprig (optional)

Cut bell peppers lengthwise into ½-inch-wide strips. Heat oil in a wide frying pan over medium heat. Add bell peppers and cook, stirring, until tender (about 8 minutes). Stir in chopped basil. Season to taste with salt and pepper. Serve hot, room temperature, or chilled.

If made ahead, cover and let stand for up to 6 hours or refrigerate for up to a day. Garnish with fresh basil. Makes 4 to 6 servings.

Per serving: 49 calories, .31 g protein, 2 g carbohydrates, 5 g total fat, 0 mg cholesterol, 1 mg sodium

Wilted Spinach with Parmesan & Pepper

2 quarts firmly packed rinsed, drained, and stemmed spinach leaves
1 tablespoon butter or margarine, diced
¼ cup grated or shredded Parmesan cheese
Coarsely ground pepper

Place moist spinach leaves in a shallow 2- to 3-quart casserole; dot with butter. Cover and bake in a 450° oven until leaves are wilted (12 to 15 minutes). Lightly mix spinach with 2 forks until coated with butter. Pass cheese and pepper to add to taste. Makes 4 servings.

Per serving: 76 calories, 6 g protein, 5 g carbohydrates, 5 g total fat, 12 mg cholesterol, 222 mg sodium

Curried Garbanzos

3 tablespoons salad oil
1 large onion, finely chopped
3 cloves garlic, minced or pressed
1 tablespoon minced fresh ginger
1 large tomato, chopped
1½ teaspoons ground cumin
1 teaspoon ground coriander
½ teaspoon *each* ground red pepper (cayenne) and ground turmeric
2 cans (about 1 lb. *each*) garbanzos, drained
¾ cup water
2 large limes
¼ cup chopped fresh cilantro (coriander) leaves (optional)

Combine oil, onion, garlic, and ginger in a wide frying pan. Cook over medium heat, stirring often, until onion is lightly browned. Add tomato and cook, stirring, until most of the liquid has evaporated. Add cumin, ground coriander, red pepper, and turmeric. Reduce heat to low and stir until spices become aromatic (3 to 5 minutes).

Add garbanzos and water. Cover and simmer, stirring occasionally, until sauce is thickened (about 20 minutes). Stir in juice from half a lime. Pour mixture into a bowl and sprinkle with chopped cilantro, if desired. Cut remaining lime into wedges and offer alongside. Makes 4 to 6 servings.

Per serving: 197 calories, 7 g protein, 23 g carbohydrates, 9 g total fat, 0 mg cholesterol, 407 mg sodium

Oven-browned Eggplant with Herbs

1 large eggplant (about 1½ lbs.), unpeeled
3 tablespoons olive oil or salad oil
2 teaspoons dry basil, oregano, rosemary, or thyme
1 clove garlic, minced or pressed
Salt and pepper

Slice eggplant crosswise about ½ inch thick. Mix oil, basil, and garlic and lightly brush over cut surfaces of eggplant.

Place eggplant in a single layer in a shallow baking pan. Bake, uncovered, in a 425° oven until eggplant is browned and very soft when pressed (25 to 40 minutes); turn, if necessary, to brown evenly. Season with salt and pepper to taste. Makes 4 servings.

Per serving: 137 calories, 2 g protein, 11 g carbohydrates, 10 g total fat, 0 mg cholesterol, 7 mg sodium

Green Beans with Bacon & Tomato Dressing

4 slices bacon
1 pound green beans
6 tablespoons catsup
¼ cup white wine vinegar

In a medium-size frying pan, cook bacon over medium heat until crisp. Lift out, drain, and crumble; set aside. Reserve drippings in pan and set aside.

In a 5- to 6-quart pan, bring 3 quarts of water to a boil over high heat. Add beans and cook just until tender-crisp (4 to 5 minutes); drain. Use hot; or, to serve cold, immerse in ice water, then drain.

Add catsup and vinegar to drippings in pan and stir over medium heat just until blended. Use hot; or let cool and use cold.

Spoon dressing onto 4 individual salad plates. Add beans and sprinkle with bacon. Makes 4 servings.

Per serving: 190 calories, 5 g protein, 15 g carbohydrates, 13 g total fat, 15 mg cholesterol, 431 mg sodium

Poultry

*Mellowed by gentle cooking, whole garlic
cloves infuse simmered drumsticks and red-skinned
potatoes with their distinctive flavor. Garlic Chicken & Potatoes (recipe on page 66) is
based on a French classic.*

Whether dashing through last-minute shopping or planning a few days ahead, today's cook usually stops at the poultry counter. Chicken comes virtually oven or pan ready, in various configurations—cut up or whole, on the bone or already boned and skinned. Another boon to the busy cook is boneless turkey breast and ground turkey, both of which translate into delectable dishes requiring little time or fuss. Besides convenience, today's poultry also offers top nutritional value at moderate prices and great versatility in cooking.

Hazelnut Chicken

PREPARATION TIME   COOKING TIME

Toasted, finely ground hazelnuts cloak moist, boneless chicken breasts. Cook the breasts briefly, just until crisp on the outside and succulent within. Serve with a colorful accompaniment of steamed baby carrots and blanched Chinese pea pods.

- ½ cup hazelnuts (filberts)
- 1 egg white
- 2 tablespoons Dijon mustard
- 2 whole chicken breasts (about 1 lb. *each*), skinned, boned, and split
  White pepper
  All-purpose flour
- 2 tablespoons fine dry bread crumbs
- 1 tablespoon butter or margarine
- 1 tablespoon salad oil
- 2 tablespoons dry white wine
- ½ cup whipping cream
  Watercress sprigs

Spread hazelnuts in a shallow baking pan and toast in a 350° oven until skins begin to split (8 to 10 minutes). Let cool slightly.

Meanwhile, beat egg white with 1 tablespoon of the mustard in a shallow bowl. Season chicken lightly with white pepper and dust with flour; set aside.

In a blender or food processor, whirl hazelnuts until finely ground; mix with bread crumbs in another shallow pan. Dip chicken in egg white mixture to coat lightly; then coat with hazelnut mixture.

In a wide frying pan, melt butter with oil over medium heat. Add chicken and cook, turning once, until browned on both sides and meat in thickest part is no longer pink when slashed (10 to 12 minutes total). Lift out chicken, reserving drippings in pan, and arrange on a warm serving dish; keep warm.

Stir wine, cream, and remaining 1 tablespoon mustard into pan. Boil over high heat, stirring constantly, until slightly thickened. Drizzle over chicken. Garnish with watercress. Makes 4 servings.

Per serving: 389 calories, 29 g protein, 9 g carbohydrates, 27 g total fat, 104 mg cholesterol, 369 mg sodium

Chicken Breasts La Jolla

PREPARATION TIME   COOKING TIME

California's much prized avocado distinguishes this dish. For an attractive presentation, arrange avocado slices alternately with chicken pieces. Serve rice or baked potatoes to take full advantage of the sauce.

- 1 large avocado
- 4 tablespoons lemon juice
- 2 tablespoons butter or margarine
- 2 cloves garlic, minced or pressed
- 2 whole chicken breasts (about 1 lb. *each*), skinned, boned, and split
  Salt and pepper
- 1 cup whipping cream
- 3 tablespoons dry vermouth
  Paprika
- ¼ cup finely chopped fresh cilantro (coriander)

Pit and peel avocado; thinly slice lengthwise. Place in a small shallow bowl and coat with 3 tablespoons of the lemon juice.

In a wide frying pan, melt butter over medium heat; add garlic and cook, stirring, until soft (about 2 minutes).

Season chicken breasts with salt and pepper to taste. Add chicken to pan and cook over medium-high heat, turning once, until lightly browned on both sides (7 to 8 minutes total). Lift out chicken, reserving drippings in pan, and transfer to a shallow 1½- to 2-quart baking dish.

To pan add remaining 1 tablespoon lemon juice, lemon juice drained from avocados, cream, and vermouth. Boil over high heat, stirring often, until reduced to about ⅔ cup (about 5 minutes).

Arrange avocado slices between chicken pieces; pour sauce evenly over both. Sprinkle with paprika and cilantro. Bake, uncovered, in a 350° oven until sauce is bubbly (10 to 12 minutes). Makes 4 servings.

Per serving: 455 calories, 28 g protein, 9 g carbohydrates, 35 g total fat, 145 mg cholesterol, 160 mg sodium

Chutney Chicken Breasts

PREPARATION TIME **10** MINUTES **18** MINUTES BAKING TIME

Chutney, rum, and slivered almonds transform plain baked chicken into flavorful company fare. Complete the menu with wild or brown rice and steamed green beans.

- 2 **tablespoons rum**
- 3 **tablespoons butter or margarine, melted**
  About ⅓ cup fine dry seasoned bread crumbs
- 3 **whole chicken breasts (about 1 lb. *each*), skinned, boned, and split**
- 1 **jar (9 oz.) Major Grey's chutney, chopped**
- 2 **tablespoons slivered almonds**
  Hot cooked wild or brown rice

Combine rum and butter in a shallow pan. Spread bread crumbs on wax paper.

Cup each chicken breast in palm of your hand, skinned side down. Fill cavity with about 1 tablespoon of the chutney and 1 teaspoon of the almonds. Fold and roll chicken around filling to enclose. Dip each piece in rum mixture, then crumbs, coating well on all sides. Place, skinned sides up, in a 9- by 13-inch baking pan. Drizzle with any remaining rum mixture.

Bake, uncovered, in a 425° oven until meat in thickest part is no longer pink when slashed (15 to 18 minutes). Spoon pan drippings over chicken. Serve with rice and remaining chutney. Makes 6 servings.

Per serving of chicken: 252 calories, 27 g protein, 16 g carbohydrates, 9 g total fat, 79 mg cholesterol, 339 mg sodium

---

Buying & Storing Fresh Poultry

When you buy fresh chicken or turkey, get it into the refrigerator or freezer as quickly as you can. Poultry products should never stand at room temperature for long periods. Plan to cook fresh poultry within 3 days of purchase; if you can't use it that soon, freeze it. Enclosed securely in heavy foil, freezer paper, or freezer-thickness plastic bags, poultry can be kept frozen for up to 6 months.

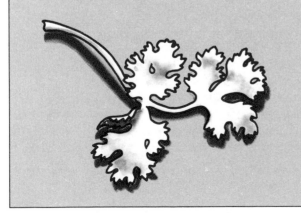

Brandied Chicken Breasts with Pears

PREPARATION TIME **10** MINUTES   **25** MINUTES COOKING TIME

A blaze of pear brandy, smoothed by a touch of cream, finishes this quick and subtly spiced sautéed chicken. Present asparagus spears or whole green beans as a tempting accompaniment.

- 3 **whole chicken breasts (about 1 lb. *each*), skinned, boned, and split**
  Salt and ground allspice
- 2 **tablespoons butter or margarine**
- 2 **green onions (including tops), thinly sliced**
- 1 **teaspoon Dijon mustard**
- ⅓ **cup regular-strength chicken broth**
- 2 **medium-size pears, peeled, cored, and cut into thin wedges**
- ¼ **cup pear brandy or brandy**
- ⅓ **cup whipping cream**

Season chicken with salt and allspice to taste. In a wide frying pan, melt butter over medium-high heat. Add chicken and cook, turning once, until golden brown on both sides. Add onions, mustard, and broth. Reduce heat, cover, and simmer for 10 minutes.

Add pear wedges, cover, and continue cooking just until pears are tender (6 to 8 minutes). Pour in brandy; set aflame (*not* beneath an exhaust fan or near flammable items), shaking pan until flames die. Lift out chicken and pears, reserving liquid in pan, and arrange on a warm serving dish; keep warm.

Add cream to pan. Boil over high heat, stirring often, until sauce is slightly thickened (2 to 3 minutes). Pour over chicken and pears. Makes 6 servings.

Per serving: 240 calories, 26 g protein, 12 g carbohydrates, 10 g total fat, 88 mg cholesterol, 195 mg sodium

Cinder Chicken Breasts

PREPARATION TIME **5** MINUTES **15** MINUTES BAKING TIME

Named for their unusual appearance, these chicken breasts look as if they've had a close encounter with barbecue coals. Actually, black sesame seeds give them a delicious crust that seals in their succulence. Look for black sesame seeds (which taste very similar to the light-colored kind) in Asian markets or in the Oriental section of your supermarket.

- ½ **cup black sesame seeds**
- 2 **whole chicken breasts (about 1 lb. *each*), skinned, boned, and split**
- 2 **tablespoons butter or margarine**
- 2 **tablespoons soy sauce**
  Lemon wedges

Spread sesame seeds thickly in center of a large sheet of wax paper. Turn chicken pieces, one at a time, in seeds, patting seeds to coat solidly; shake off excess.

Place chicken in a single layer in a 9- by 13-inch baking dish. Bake, uncovered, in a 400° oven until meat in thickest part is no longer pink when slashed (about 15 minutes).

Meanwhile, in a small pan, melt butter over medium heat and stir in soy sauce. Garnish chicken with lemon and serve with soy sauce mixture. Makes 4 servings.

Per serving: 280 calories, 29 g protein, 5 g carbohydrates, 16 g total fat, 79 mg cholesterol, 646 mg sodium

Honey-baked Chicken

PREPARATION TIME **8** MINUTES **20** MINUTES BAKING TIME

Delicate sesame seeds add crunch to these glazed, tart-sweet chicken breasts. Offer carrots and hot steamed rice to share the flavorful sauce.

- 2 **tablespoons sesame seeds**
- 3 **tablespoons honey**
- ¼ **cup Dijon mustard**
- ¼ **cup dry sherry or dry white wine**
- 1 **tablespoon lemon juice**
- 3 **whole chicken breasts (about 1 lb. *each*), skinned, boned, and split**

Toast sesame seeds in a small frying pan over medium heat, shaking pan frequently, until golden (about 5 minutes). Transfer sesame seeds to a small bowl and blend with honey, mustard, sherry, and lemon juice.

Arrange chicken breasts, slightly apart, in a 9- by 13-inch baking dish or pan; pour sesame seed mixture evenly over chicken. Bake, uncovered, in a 400° oven, basting several times with sesame seed mixture, until meat in thickest part is no longer pink when slashed (15 to 20 minutes).

Lift out chicken and transfer to a platter or plates. Pour sauce into a small bowl to pass at the table. Makes 6 servings.

Per serving: 185 calories, 26 g protein, 12 g carbohydrates, 4 g total fat, 63 mg cholesterol, 369 mg sodium

Crumb-coated Dijon Chicken

PREPARATION TIME **10** MINUTES **15** MINUTES BAKING TIME

Called *panko* in Japan, coarse dried bread crumbs give chicken breasts a savory, crunchy coating. To carry out the Oriental theme, serve with a salad of sliced cucumber that's been marinated in seasoned rice vinegar with ginger.

- 2 **tablespoons butter or margarine, melted**
- 2 **tablespoons Dijon mustard**
- 1 **clove garlic, minced or pressed**
- ¼ **cup panko (Japanese-style bread crumbs)**
- 1 **tablespoon *each* grated Parmesan cheese and minced parsley**
- 2 **whole chicken breasts (about 1 lb. *each*), skinned, boned, and split**
  Dijon Sauce (recipe follows)

In a wide, shallow bowl, blend butter, mustard, and garlic. In another bowl, mix panko, cheese, and parsley.

Dip chicken in butter mixture to coat; then dip skinned side of each piece in panko mixture. Place chicken in a single layer, crumb sides up, in a shallow rimmed baking pan.

Bake, uncovered, in a 500° oven until crumbs are golden and meat in thickest part is no longer pink when slashed (about 15 minutes). Meanwhile, prepare Dijon Sauce. Serve breasts whole or cut crosswise into thick slices. Accompany with sauce. Makes 4 servings.

Dijon Sauce. Mix ¼ cup **mayonnaise** and 2 tablespoons **Dijon mustard**.

Per serving of chicken: 211 calories, 27 g protein, 6 g carbohydrates, 8 g total fat, 80 mg cholesterol, 422 mg sodium

Per tablespoon of sauce: 72 calories, .10 g protein, .99 g carbohydrate, 8 g total fat, 5 mg cholesterol, 200 mg sodium

Herbed Chicken with Artichokes

PREPARATION TIME **10** MINUTES   **25** MINUTES BAKING TIME

Though it looks like a day-long effort, this hearty baked chicken dish is quite easy to prepare and needs little in the way of accompaniments—just a simple salad and a loaf of crusty bread.

> 3 **whole chicken breasts (about 1 lb. *each*), skinned, boned, and split**
> 1 **jar (6 oz.) marinated artichoke hearts, drained**
> ¼ **cup butter or margarine**
> ¼ **pound mushrooms, thinly sliced**
> 1 **clove garlic, minced or pressed**
> 1 **can (8 oz.) tomato sauce**
> ½ **teaspoon *each* dry basil, dry oregano, and ground turmeric**
> **Paprika**
> **Sour cream (optional)**

Arrange chicken in a 9- by 13-inch baking dish; tuck artichokes between chicken pieces. In a wide frying pan, melt butter over medium-high heat; drizzle half the butter over chicken, reserving remainder in pan. Bake chicken, uncovered, in a 375° oven for 10 minutes.

Meanwhile, add mushrooms to pan and cook, stirring often, until soft. Add garlic and cook, stirring often, for about 1 minute. Stir in tomato sauce, basil, oregano, and turmeric. Bring to a boil; set aside.

Pour mushroom mixture over chicken; sprinkle with paprika. Return to oven and continue baking until meat in thickest part is no longer pink when slashed (10 to 15 more minutes). Offer sour cream, if desired, to add to individual portions. Makes 6 servings.

Per serving: 235 calories, 27 g protein, 6 g carbohydrates, 12 g total fat, 84 mg cholesterol, 406 mg sodium

To Microwave: Arrange chicken and artichokes in microwave-safe baking dish as directed. Cover with plastic wrap. Microwave on **HIGH (100%)** for 5 minutes. Rotate chicken pieces so uncooked portions are toward outside of dish; set aside.

Reduce butter to 2 tablespoons; place in a shallow microwave-safe baking dish. Microwave, uncovered, on **HIGH (100%)** for 1½ minutes. Stir in mushrooms and garlic; microwave, uncovered, on **HIGH (100%)** for 3 minutes. Stir in tomato sauce, basil, oregano, and turmeric and pour over chicken. Microwave, uncovered, on **HIGH (100%)** for 6 to 8 minutes, rotating dish once or twice, until meat in thickest part is no longer pink when slashed. Sprinkle with paprika and serve with sour cream, if desired.

Chicken Breasts au Poivre

(Pictured on facing page)

PREPARATION TIME **8** MINUTES   **10** MINUTES COOKING TIME

Peppercorns—both pink and black—add two-tone excitement to these sautéed chicken breasts. The familiar black peppercorns deliver the more potent flavor. The pink ones, from an ornamental tree, have milder heat and a sweet-hot, flowery impact. Sold canned in brine or freeze-dried in specialty shops, pink peppercorns are a new ingredient for many people. They may cause allergic reactions to some, so start out cautiously.

> 2 **whole chicken breasts (about 1 lb. *each*), skinned, boned, and split**
> 1 **teaspoon crushed black peppercorns**
> 4 **teaspoons crushed pink peppercorns**
> 2 **to 3 tablespoons butter or margarine**
> ½ **cup Madeira or dry sherry**
> ½ **cup whipping cream**
> 1 **teaspoon fresh rosemary leaves or** ¼ **teaspoon slightly crushed dry rosemary**
> **Rosemary sprigs (optional)**

Place chicken breasts between sheets of plastic wrap. With a flat-surfaced mallet, pound chicken until about ¼ inch thick. Sprinkle each side with ⅛ teaspoon of the black peppercorns and ½ teaspoon of the pink peppercorns; lightly pound peppercorns into chicken.

In a wide frying pan, melt 2 tablespoons of the butter over high heat. Add chicken breasts; do not crowd. Cook, turning once, until meat in thickest part is no longer pink when slashed (about 1 minute total). Lift out and transfer to a warm platter; keep warm. Repeat until all chicken is cooked, adding butter as needed.

Stir Madeira into pan, scraping browned bits free. Add cream and rosemary leaves. Boil, stirring often, until reduced by half. Pour over chicken. Garnish with rosemary sprigs, if desired. Makes 4 servings.

Per serving: 301 calories, 26 g protein, 5 g carbohydrates, 19 g total fat, 120 mg cholesterol, 171 mg sodium

Generously coated with both black and
pink peppercorns, pounded Chicken Breasts au Poivre (recipe
on facing page) create an elegant entrée with spring-fresh asparagus alongside. Sautéing
reduces the peppers' heat, accentuating their spiciness instead.

*Plump chicken paupiettes, nestled on a
bed of watercress, offer both a creamy interior and a
savory garnish. To accompany Blue Cheese-stuffed Chicken with Walnuts (recipe on facing page),
serve crisp French-fried shoestring potatoes.*

Broiled Chicken & Cheese Mexicana

PREPARATION TIME **15** MINUTES   **15** MINUTES BROILING TIME

This saladlike Mexican main dish features cheese-gilded chicken, festively flavored with lime, garlic, and red pepper. As summertime companions, add ice-cold beer and hot, buttery corn on the cob.

- **6 boneless chicken thighs (about 1¼ lbs. *total*), skinned**
- **2 tablespoons lime or lemon juice**
- **1 tablespoon red wine vinegar**
- **2 tablespoons olive oil or salad oil**
- **1 clove garlic, minced or pressed**
- **⅛ teaspoon *each* salt, ground cumin, and crushed red pepper**
  About 3 cups shredded iceberg lettuce
- **1 medium-size avocado**
- **½ cup *each* shredded jack and sharp Cheddar cheeses**
- **1 medium-size tomato, cut into wedges**
  Lime wedges (optional)
  Fresh cilantro (coriander) sprigs (optional)

Place chicken thighs between sheets of plastic wrap. With a flat-surfaced mallet, gently pound until thighs are about ¼ inch thick. Mix lime juice, vinegar, oil, garlic, salt, cumin, and red pepper until well combined. Brush chicken on both sides with lime juice mixture; set remaining mixture aside.

Place chicken, skinned sides down, on rack of a broiler pan. Broil about 4 inches below heat, turning once and brushing with some of the lime juice mixture, until meat in thickest part is no longer pink when slashed (12 to 15 minutes total).

Meanwhile, spread lettuce on a serving platter. Pit, peel, and slice avocado; brush with some of the remaining lime juice mixture.

Sprinkle chicken with jack and Cheddar cheeses; return to oven and broil until cheese is melted (1½ to 2 minutes). Drizzle any remaining lime juice mixture over lettuce. Arrange chicken, avocado, and tomato on lettuce. Garnish with lime and cilantro, if desired. Makes 3 servings.

Per serving: 542 calories, 42 g protein, 10 g carbohydrates, 38 g total fat, 166 mg cholesterol, 462 mg sodium

Blue Cheese-stuffed Chicken with Walnuts

(Pictured on facing page)

PREPARATION TIME **12** MINUTES   **25** MINUTES COOKING TIME

As these tender chicken paupiettes simmer, nuggets of blue cheese inside them melt, enriching the creamy wine sauce. Crisp, buttery walnuts—a delectable complement for the cheese—add the last, luxuriant touch. Who would ever guess that such an elegant entrée could be so easy and quick to prepare? Just add French fries, as shown in the photograph, or a green salad and sliced baguette.

- **6 boneless chicken thighs (about 1¼ lbs. *total*), skinned**
- **6 sticks (½ by 2 inches *each*) blue-veined cheese (about 3 oz. *total*)**
  All-purpose flour
- **1 tablespoon butter or margarine**
- **1 tablespoon salad oil**
- **½ cup coarsely chopped walnuts**
- **½ cup dry white wine or chicken broth**
- **½ cup whipping cream**
  Watercress sprigs

Place chicken thighs between sheets of plastic wrap. With a flat-surfaced mallet, pound until thighs are about ¼ inch thick. With thighs placed skinned sides down, put a stick of cheese at one end of each. Fold in sides and roll up compactly; fasten securely with skewers or wooden picks. Dust with flour.

In a wide frying pan, melt butter with oil over medium heat. Add walnuts and cook, stirring occasionally, until lightly browned (2 to 3 minutes). With a slotted spoon, remove nuts from pan and set aside, reserving drippings in pan.

Add chicken to pan; cook until lightly browned on all sides (about 5 minutes). Pour in wine. Reduce heat, cover, and simmer until meat is no longer pink when slashed (12 to 15 minutes). Lift out chicken, reserving liquid in pan, and arrange on a warm platter; keep warm.

Stir cream into pan. Boil over high heat, stirring often, until reduced by about half. Pour sauce over chicken; sprinkle with walnuts. Garnish with watercress. Makes 3 servings.

Per serving: 580 calories, 41 g protein, 9 g carbohydrates, 43 g total fat, 205 mg cholesterol, 586 mg sodium

Cook-ahead Poultry

When time is short, having cooked chicken or turkey in the refrigerator is almost like having money in the bank—it always comes in handy, whether you're planning a casserole, a salad, sandwiches, or some other quick family favorite.

Roasting a whole chicken or two or such sizable turkey pieces as a breast half or thigh is well worth your time, since they'll often yield enough meat for at least two meals.

Below are directions for roasting poultry the traditional way. For exceptionally moist and smooth-textured poultry, try the gentle cooking method we call steeping (see below, right).

Roasting Chicken or Turkey

Select a **frying chicken** (3 to 4 lbs.), roasting chicken (5 to 6 lbs.), whole turkey (8 to 15 lbs.), turkey breast half (bone in or boneless, 2 to 4 lbs.), or turkey thigh (1 to 1½ lbs.).

If roasting a whole bird, remove neck and giblets from body cavity; reserve for other uses, if desired. Rinse bird inside and out, and pat dry. If desired, place **lemon wedges** and **parsley sprigs** or other fresh herbs in cavity.

Place whole bird, breast side up (for turkey pieces, skin side up), on a rack in a shallow roasting pan. Brush lightly with melted **butter** or margarine or spray with vegetable oil cooking spray. For a whole bird, insert a meat thermometer in thickest part of thigh (not touching bone); for turkey breast, insert thermometer in thickest part.

Approximate roasting times and temperatures are as follows:

Frying chicken: 17 to 20 minutes per pound; 375° oven; thermometer reading, 185°F

Roasting chicken: 20 to 25 minutes per pound; 350° oven; thermometer reading, 185°F

Turkey: 15 minutes per pound; 325° oven; thermometer reading, 185°F

Turkey breast: 20 minutes per pound; 350° oven; thermometer reading, 170°F

Turkey thigh: 60 minutes per pound; 350° oven; thermometer reading, 185°F

Steeped Chicken Breasts

Split 2 whole **chicken breasts** (2 lbs. *total*); place in a wide 4- to 5-quart pan. Pour in enough water to cover chicken by 1 to 2 inches. Lift out chicken. Add 2 or 3 thin **lemon slices;** cover and bring water to a rolling boil over high heat. Remove from heat and quickly immerse chicken.

Cover pan tightly and let steep for 20 minutes; do *not* uncover until time is up. Chicken is done when meat in thickest part is no longer pink when slashed. If not done, return to pan, cover, and let steep until done.

Drain chicken, let cool in ice water, and drain again; pat dry. Skin and bone chicken. If made ahead, cover and refrigerate for up to 2 days.

Steeped Turkey Breast

Place a 2½- to 3-pound **turkey breast half** in a 6- to 8-quart pan. Pour in enough water to cover turkey by 1 to 2 inches. Lift out turkey. Add 3 or 4 **parsley sprigs;** cover and bring water to a rolling boil over high heat. Add turkey, cover, and immediately turn heat to very low. Cook for 20 minutes. Remove from heat (do *not* uncover); let steep for 1 to 1½ hours.

Remove turkey from pan; turkey is done when meat in thickest part is no longer pink when slashed. If not done, cover turkey. Then cover pan, bring water to a simmer, and remove from heat. Add turkey, cover, and steep until done. Drain, let cool in ice water, and drain again; pat dry.

Skin and bone turkey. If made ahead, cover and refrigerate for up to 2 days.

Mustard Chicken Chunks with Vermicelli

PREPARATION TIME **13** MINUTES   **20** MINUTES COOKING TIME

Tender chicken morsels make a delectable foil for the distinctive flavors of Dijon mustard and crunchy mustard seeds. Spoon the combination over hot vermicelli or another pasta of your choice. For a touch of color, serve with sliced carrots, buttered and nutmeg dusted.

> 1¼ to 1½ **pounds boneless chicken thighs, skinned**
> 1 **tablespoon butter or margarine**
> 1 **tablespoon olive oil or salad oil**
> 1 **small clove garlic, minced or pressed**
> 1 **teaspoon mustard seeds, coarsely crushed**
> ¼ **teaspoon dry tarragon**
> ⅓ **cup dry white wine**
> 6 **ounces vermicelli or other pasta**
> 2 **teaspoons Dijon mustard**
> 4 **tablespoons thinly sliced green onions (including tops)**
> ½ **cup sour cream**

Cut chicken into bite-size chunks. In a wide frying pan, melt butter with oil over medium-high heat. Add chicken; cook, stirring often, until browned on all sides (about 5 minutes). Stir in garlic, mustard seeds, tarragon, and wine. Reduce heat, cover, and simmer until meat is no longer pink when slashed (8 to 10 minutes). Meanwhile, following package directions, cook pasta in boiling salted water until *al dente*.

Add Dijon mustard and 3 tablespoons of the onions to chicken. Cook over medium-high heat, stirring often, until most of the liquid has evaporated. Remove from heat and stir in sour cream until smoothly combined. Serve over hot cooked vermicelli. Sprinkle with remaining 1 tablespoon onions. Makes 4 servings.

Per serving: 453 calories, 34 g protein, 35 g carbohydrates, 19 g total fat, 136 mg cholesterol, 241 mg sodium

To Microwave: Prepare chicken as directed. Omit oil. Combine chicken, butter, garlic, mustard seeds, and tarragon in a 9- to 10-inch round microwave-safe dish. Microwave, covered, on **HIGH (100%),** for 6 to 8 minutes, stirring once, until chicken is no longer pink when slashed. Lift out chicken, reserving liquid in dish. Reduce wine to ¼ cup. Stir wine and mustard into dish. Microwave, uncovered, on **HIGH (100%)**

for 5 to 8 minutes or until mixture boils and edges brown slightly. Meanwhile, cook pasta as directed.

Return chicken to dish; stir in the 3 tablespoons onions and sour cream. Microwave, uncovered, on **MEDIUM (50%)** for 1 to 2 minutes or just until heated through. Stir; serve as directed.

Chicken Legs in Cassis

PREPARATION TIME **3** MINUTES   **42** MINUTES COOKING TIME

In Europe, fruit is a favorite accent for meats and poultry. Here, dried currants, black currant vinegar, and cassis—three forms of the same fruit—embellish dark meat of chicken with their sweet-tart distinction. Serve with oven-crisp French fries and a salad of watercress and lettuce.

> 4 **whole chicken legs, thighs attached (1½ to 2 lbs. *total*)**
>   **Salt, white pepper, and ground nutmeg**
> 2 **tablespoons butter or margarine**
> 1 **tablespoon salad oil**
> 1 **clove garlic, minced or pressed**
> 2 **tablespoons cassis vinegar or raspberry wine vinegar**
> 2 **teaspoons tomato paste**
> ¼ **cup dried currants**
> ¾ **cup regular-strength chicken broth**
> ¼ **cup *each* dry white wine and crème de cassis (black currant liqueur)**
> 1 **tablespoon all-purpose flour**

Season chicken with salt, white pepper, and nutmeg to taste. In a wide frying pan, melt 1 tablespoon of the butter with oil over medium-high heat. Add chicken and cook, turning once, until browned on both sides (10 to 12 minutes). Stir in garlic, vinegar, and tomato paste; sprinkle with currants. Pour in broth, wine, and crème de cassis. Bring to a boil; reduce heat, cover, and simmer until meat near thighbone is no longer pink when slashed (about 25 minutes).

Meanwhile, mix remaining 1 tablespoon butter smoothly with flour; set aside. Lift out chicken, reserving drippings in pan, and transfer to an ovenproof platter or shallow casserole; place in a 400° oven while completing sauce. Boil liquid in frying pan over high heat, stirring often, until reduced by about a third. Blend in butter-flour mixture a little at a time, stirring constantly with a whisk, until sauce is thickened and shiny. Pour over chicken. Makes 4 servings.

Per serving: 403 calories, 30 g protein, 14 g carbohydrates, 24 g total fat, 119 mg cholesterol, 369 mg sodium

Santa Fe Chicken Drumsticks with Rice

PREPARATION TIME 7 MINUTES   38 MINUTES BAKING TIME

Brightened with bits of onion and bacon, a bed of fluffy rice absorbs the chili-seasoned juices of these baked drumsticks. For cool contrast, add green beans and an avocado salad.

- 2 **tablespoons butter or margarine**
- 1 **tablespoon salad oil**
- ⅓ **cup all-purpose flour**
- 1 **teaspoon chili powder**
- ½ **teaspoon paprika**
- ¼ **teaspoon pepper**
- 8 **small chicken drumsticks (1½ to 2 lbs. *total*)**
  Onion Rice (recipe follows)
  Chopped parsley

Combine butter and oil in a shallow rimmed baking pan. Set in a 400° oven until butter is melted. Meanwhile, combine flour, chili powder, paprika, and pepper in a small bag. Add drumsticks, about half at a time, shaking until lightly coated with seasoned flour. Arrange in a single layer in pan, turning to coat with butter mixture.

Bake, uncovered, in a 400° oven until drumsticks are well browned and meat near bone is no longer pink when slashed (35 to 40 minutes). Meanwhile, prepare Onion Rice.

Arrange chicken and rice on a warm platter; garnish with parsley. Makes 4 servings.

Onion Rice. In a medium-size frying pan, cook 2 slices **bacon,** diced, over medium heat until fat is melted. Add ⅓ cup chopped **onion** and ⅔ cup **long-grain white rice;** cook, stirring, until rice is lightly browned (about 5 minutes). Add ⅔ cup *each* **regular-strength chicken broth** and **water.** Bring to a boil; reduce heat, cover, and simmer until rice is tender to bite and liquid is absorbed (about 20 minutes).

Per serving: 544 calories, 34 g protein, 36 g carbohydrates, 28 g total fat, 121 mg cholesterol, 410 mg sodium

Cumin Drumsticks with Curried Rice

Follow directions for Santa Fe Chicken Drumsticks with Rice but omit paprika and pepper. To flour mixture add ½ teaspoon **ground cumin;** increase chili powder to 1½ teaspoons.

Omit bacon and chopped onion from Onion Rice. Heat 1 tablespoon **salad oil** over medium heat. Add rice and ¾ teaspoon **curry powder** and cook, stirring, until rice begins to look opaque (3 to 5 minutes). Add ¼ cup **golden raisins** with broth and water. Just before serving, stir in ⅓ cup sliced **green onions** (including tops).

Garlic Chicken & Potatoes

(Pictured on page 54)

PREPARATION TIME 8 MINUTES   37 MINUTES COOKING TIME

To fully absorb the delicious impact of its garlic, serve this entrée with a loaf of crusty bread and a salad of tender butter lettuce. Inspired by the cooking of Provence, it's a slightly less exuberant rendition of the classic Chicken with 40 Cloves of Garlic.

- 3 **tablespoons olive oil or salad oil**
- 4 **whole chicken legs, thighs attached (1½ to 2 lbs. *total*)**
- 8 **small red thin-skinned potatoes (1½ to 2 inches in diameter)**
- 1 **teaspoon dry rosemary**
- ¼ **cup water**
- 24 **large cloves garlic, peeled and slightly crushed**
  Salt and pepper
  Rosemary sprigs (optional)

Heat oil in a wide frying pan over medium-high heat. Add chicken and potatoes; cook, turning potatoes occasionally and chicken once, until chicken pieces are browned on both sides (10 to 12 minutes total).

Reduce heat to low and add dry rosemary and water. Cover and cook for 15 minutes. Turn chicken again and add garlic. Cover and continue cooking, turning potatoes and garlic occasionally, until potatoes are tender and meat near thighbone is no longer pink when slashed (about 10 more minutes). Lift out chicken, potatoes, and garlic, reserving drippings in pan, and transfer to a serving platter.

Stir pan drippings, scraping browned bits free; pour over chicken and vegetables. Season with salt and pepper to taste. Garnish with rosemary sprigs, if desired. Makes 4 servings.

Per serving: 451 calories, 32 g protein, 23 g carbohydrates, 25 g total fat, 103 mg cholesterol, 107 mg sodium

*The flash-in-a-pan method may remind you
of Chinese cooking. But bringing together coconut milk,
fresh basil, and fiery bursts of crushed red pepper reveals the true origin of
Thai Chicken & Basil Stir-fry (recipe on page 61).*

Chicken Thighs Provençale

PREPARATION TIME **5** MINUTES **25** MINUTES COOKING TIME

Though the choreographed ingredients come from the south of France, the quick tempo of this recipe is definitely American. To speed their cooking time, chop the chicken thighs into shorter pieces. Serve a pasta, such as tagliarini, to show off the anise-flavored sauce.

- 6 **chicken thighs (2 to 2¼ lbs. *total*)**
- 2 **tablespoons olive oil**
  Salt and pepper
- 2 **tablespoons Pernod, anisette, or brandy**
- 1 **small onion, finely chopped**
- 2 **cloves garlic, minced or pressed**
- 1 **teaspoon herbes de Provence or ¼ teaspoon *each* dry basil, oregano, thyme, and marjoram**
- 1 **tablespoon all-purpose flour**
- ½ **cup dry white wine**
- 1 **can (16 oz.) diced tomatoes in purée**
- ¼ **cup Niçoise or small ripe olives**

With a cleaver or heavy knife, cut each thigh in half through bone. Heat oil in a wide frying pan over medium-high heat. Add chicken pieces and cook, turning once, until browned on both sides and meat near bone is no longer pink when slashed (15 to 20 minutes total). Season with salt and pepper to taste.

Pour in Pernod and set aflame (*not* beneath an exhaust fan or near flammable items), shaking pan until flames die. Lift out chicken pieces and set aside. Discard all but 1 tablespoon of the drippings.

Add onion, garlic, and herbs to pan and cook, stirring often, until onion is lightly browned. Sprinkle in flour and cook, stirring, until bubbly. Blend in wine and bring to a boil. Add tomatoes and their liquid and bring to a simmer. Stir in olives. Return chicken to pan and cook, stirring gently, just until heated through. Makes 4 servings.

Per serving: 445 calories, 36 g protein, 18 g carbohydrates, 26 g total fat, 123 mg cholesterol, 629 mg sodium

Kauai Chicken

PREPARATION TIME **5** MINUTES **40** MINUTES BAKING TIME

One of China's most admired exports, hoisin sauce traditionally accompanies Peking duck. Here it also enhances a speedy chicken dish from Hawaii.

- 8 **small chicken thighs (2 to 2½ lbs. *total*)**
- ¼ **cup *each* granulated sugar and firmly packed brown sugar**
- ⅓ **cup soy sauce**
- 2 **tablespoons hoisin sauce**
- 1 **clove garlic, minced or pressed**

Arrange chicken pieces, skin sides down, slightly apart in a single layer in a shallow rimmed baking pan or casserole. Stir together granulated sugar, brown sugar, soy sauce, hoisin sauce, and garlic. Spoon about half the mixture over chicken.

Bake, uncovered, in a 400° oven for 25 minutes. Turn chicken and add remaining sauce. Return to oven and continue baking until meat near bone is no longer pink when slashed (about 15 minutes). Makes 4 servings.

Per serving: 489 calories, 39 g protein, 30 g carbohydrates, 23 g total fat, 136 mg cholesterol, 1741 mg sodium

To Microwave: In a 9- to 10-inch round or square microwave-safe dish, stir together granulated sugar, brown sugar, soy sauce, hoisin sauce, and garlic. Arrange chicken pieces, skin sides down, in a single layer in sauce mixture and cover with plastic wrap. Microwave on **HIGH (100%)** for 10 minutes.

Turn pieces over and rotate so uncooked portions are toward outside of dish; spoon sauce over top, and cover again. Microwave on **HIGH (100%)** for 6 more minutes. Then uncover and microwave on **HIGH (100%)** for 3 more minutes. Let stand for 3 minutes; meat near bone should no longer be pink when slashed. Before serving, spoon off and discard surface fat.

Orange-Herb Chicken

PREPARATION TIME **8** MINUTES **35** MINUTES BAKING TIME

A baste of soy sauce, orange juice, and herbs lends these baked chicken pieces an appealing complexity of flavors. Offer steamed rice alongside as a foil for the assertive sauce.

- **Orange-Herb Baste (recipe follows)**
  Vegetable oil cooking spray
- 1 **frying chicken (3 to 3¼ lbs.), cut up**
- ¼ **cup regular-strength chicken broth**

Prepare Orange-Herb Baste; set aside.

Spray a 12- by 15-inch shallow baking pan with cooking spray. Setting chicken breasts aside, place remaining chicken pieces, skin sides down, in pan; spoon about a third of the baste over chicken. Bake, uncovered, in a 400° oven for 15 minutes.

Turn chicken and add breasts; spoon remaining baste over chicken. Return to oven and continue baking until meat in thickest part of breasts is no longer pink when slashed (about 20 more minutes). Lift out chicken, reserving drippings in pan, and transfer to a warm platter; keep warm.

Pour broth into baking pan, stirring to dissolve drippings; pour into a 1½- to 2-quart pan. Bring to a boil over high heat; spoon over chicken. Makes 4 servings.

Orange-Herb Baste. Mix 1 can (6 oz.) **frozen orange juice concentrate,** thawed; ⅓ cup **soy sauce;** 1½ teaspoons minced **fresh ginger** or ½ teaspoon ground ginger; 1 clove **garlic,** minced or pressed; and 1 teaspoon *each* chopped **fresh thyme, sage, marjoram, rosemary,** and **oregano leaves** or ½ teaspoon *each* of the dry herbs.

Per serving: 358 calories, 42 g protein, 23 g carbohydrates, 10 g total fat, 117 mg cholesterol, 1,537 mg sodium

Baked Chicken Quarters with Port & Grapes

PREPARATION TIME **10** MINUTES   **35** MINUTES BAKING TIME

Many of us associate elegant cuisine with time-consuming preparation—so, it's hard to believe that this exquisite dish comes to the table in such short order. Before you prepare the chicken, pop small whole sweet potatoes into the oven to serve alongside.

- 1 **frying chicken (3 to 3¼ lbs.), cut into quarters**
- 1 **tablespoon butter or margarine, melted**
 Salt and white pepper
- ¾ **cup regular-strength chicken broth**
- ½ **cup tawny port**
- 1 **tablespoon cornstarch, blended with 1 tablespoon water**
- 1 **tablespoon brown sugar**
- ⅛ **teaspoon dry thyme**
- 1½ **cups seedless red grapes**

Brush skin sides of chicken with butter; season with salt and white pepper to taste. Place, skin sides down,

in a shallow baking pan; do not crowd. Bake, uncovered, in a 400° oven for 20 minutes; turn and continue baking until chicken is crisp and browned and meat near thighbone is no longer pink when slashed (about 15 more minutes). Lift out chicken, reserving drippings in pan, and transfer to a deep serving platter; keep warm.

Pour broth into baking pan, scraping browned bits free; pour into a 2-quart pan. Add wine, cornstarch mixture, brown sugar, and thyme. Boil over high heat, stirring constantly, until mixture is thickened and clear. Add grapes, stirring just until heated through.

Pour half the sauce over and around chicken. Pass remaining sauce at the table. Makes 4 servings.

Per serving: 333 calories, 39 g protein, 13 g carbohydrates, 13 g total fat, 125 mg cholesterol, 334 mg sodium

Thawing Chicken in the Microwave

Using medium (50%) power, you can defrost frozen chicken quickly in your microwave. To thaw a frozen 3½-pound cut-up frying chicken, unwrap and place on a microwave-safe plate; cover with heavy plastic wrap or wax paper.

Microwave on **MEDIUM (50%)** for 10 minutes, turning chicken over and rotating plate a quarter turn after 5 minutes. Let stand for 10 minutes. Repeat, separating pieces as soon as possible and placing them in a single layer with meatiest portions toward outer edge. Wings should be thawed after second 10-minute period. Microwave remaining pieces on **MEDIUM (50%)** for 5 more minutes; let stand for 5 minutes. If needed, microwave on **MEDIUM (50%)** for 2 more minutes. Thawed chicken should be flexible but still very cold.

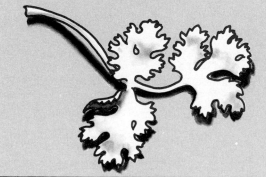

*For short-order sandwiches with spirited
south-of-the-border flavor, stack up Avocado-Chicken
Rolls (recipe on facing page). To cooked chicken, you add green chiles, avocado, melted
cheese, and a splash of your favorite salsa.*

Chicken & Green Chile Enchiladas

PREPARATION TIME **25** MINUTES   **15** MINUTES BAKING TIME

While the enchiladas are baking, prepare a simple lettuce and avocado salad. To round out a festive Mexican-style menu, serve wedges of chilled watermelon or fresh pineapple spears for dessert.

> 8 or 10 small flour tortillas (6 inches in diameter)
> 1 tablespoon salad oil
> 1 medium-size onion, thinly sliced
> ½ teaspoon ground cumin
> ¼ teaspoon dry oregano
> 1 small can (4 oz.) diced green chiles
> ½ cup whipping cream
> 3 cups diced cooked chicken
> 1 small tomato, seeded and chopped
> 2 cups (8 oz.) shredded jack cheese
> 1 cup (4 oz.) shredded Cheddar cheese
> Sour cream (optional)
> Sliced ripe olives (optional)

Dampen tortillas lightly with water; wrap in foil and place in a 350° oven until hot (12 to 15 minutes).

Meanwhile, heat oil in a wide frying pan over medium heat. Add onion, cumin, and oregano; cook, stirring often, until onion is soft (3 to 5 minutes). Stir in chiles and cream. Boil over high heat, stirring often, until thickened (about 2 minutes). Add chicken and tomato; remove from heat and stir in 1 cup of the jack cheese.

Spoon an equal amount of chicken filling on each tortilla; roll up and place, seam sides down, in a single layer in a lightly greased shallow 8- by 12-inch casserole. Sprinkle with Cheddar cheese and remaining 1 cup jack cheese.

Bake, uncovered, in a 425° oven until cheese is melted and enchiladas are heated through (12 to 15 minutes). Garnish with sour cream and olives, if desired. Makes 4 or 5 servings.

Per serving: 672 calories, 46 g protein, 29 g carbohydrates, 42 g total fat, 166 mg cholesterol, 886 mg sodium

To Microwave: In a microwave-safe 1½- to 2-quart casserole, combine oil, onion, cumin, and oregano. Microwave on **HIGH (100%)** for 5 minutes, stirring once or twice, until onion is soft. Reduce cream to ⅓ cup; add cream and microwave on **HIGH (100%)** for 3 minutes. Stir in chiles, chicken, tomato, and 1 cup of the jack cheese; set aside.

Enclose tortillas in plastic wrap or a plastic bag. Microwave on **HIGH (100%)** for 1¼ to 1½ minutes or until warm and pliable.

Fill and roll tortillas as directed. Place in a microwave-safe casserole. Sprinkle with Cheddar cheese and remaining 1 cup jack cheese. Cover loosely with plastic wrap and microwave on **HIGH (100%)** for 10 minutes, rotating casserole 2 or 3 times. Let stand for 3 minutes. Garnish as directed.

Avocado-Chicken Rolls

(Pictured on facing page)

PREPARATION TIME **15** MINUTES   **5** MINUTES BROILING TIME

Quick to put together when you have cooked chicken on hand, these multilayered sandwiches will satisfy even the heartiest appetite. Add a lively salsa to taste.

> 4 round crusty rolls (about 4 inches in diameter *each*)
> 2 tablespoons butter or margarine
> ½ cup sour cream
> 2 teaspoons Dijon mustard
> About 1½ cups shredded or sliced cooked chicken
> About ⅔ cup bottled salsa
> 4 canned whole green chiles, split open lengthwise
> 2 small avocados
> About ¼ pound jack cheese, thinly sliced

Split rolls in half and spread cut sides with butter. Place, buttered sides up, on a baking sheet. Broil about 6 inches below heat until golden (about 2 minutes). Set aside tops.

Spread bottoms of rolls with sour cream and mustard. Mix chicken with about ⅓ cup of the salsa and mound evenly on rolls; top each with a chile.

Halve, pit, and peel avocados; place cut sides down. Cut each half from wide, round end to within about 1 inch of narrow top, making slices about ¼ inch thick. Lay knife across slices and press gently to fan out. Carefully lift each avocado with a wide spatula and place on chile. Cover with cheese.

Broil 6 inches below heat until cheese is melted (about 3 minutes). Serve with tops of rolls and remaining salsa to add to taste. Makes 4 sandwiches.

Per sandwich: 634 calories, 31 g protein, 45 g carbohydrates, 38 g total fat, 102 mg cholesterol, 1251 mg sodium

Quick Paella

PREPARATION TIME **10** MINUTES   **35** MINUTES COOKING TIME

A colorful classic of Spain, paella combines chicken, sausages, and shellfish with boldly seasoned rice. Like many traditional one-pot dinners, it can take hours to cook. But we've reduced the time by using deli-roasted chicken, heat-and-serve sausages, and canned clams. Just add a crisp cabbage slaw and crusty bread.

    About ½ pound Polish sausages, sliced ¼ inch thick
1 clove garlic, minced or pressed
1 small onion, chopped
1 cup long-grain white rice
1 jar (4 oz.) sliced pimentos
1 can (6½ oz.) minced clams
1 can (14½ oz.) regular-strength chicken broth
1 cooked whole chicken (1½ to 2 lbs.), cut into serving-size pieces
1 or 2 green onions (including tops), chopped

In a wide frying pan, cook sausages briefly over medium-high heat to release some of the fat; add garlic, onion, and rice. Cook, stirring often, until onion is soft and rice turns opaque (about 4 minutes). Mix in pimentos, juice from clams (set clams aside), and broth. Bring to a boil; reduce heat to medium-low, cover, and cook until rice is barely tender to bite (about 15 minutes).

Stir clams into rice mixture and lay chicken pieces over rice. Cover and continue cooking until chicken is heated through (10 to 15 minutes).

Spread rice mixture on a platter and arrange chicken on top; sprinkle with onions. Makes 3 or 4 servings.

Per serving: 776 calories, 58 g protein, 44 g carbohydrates, 38 g total fat, 188 mg cholesterol, 1350 mg sodium

Baked Cornish Hens with Vegetables

(Pictured on page 3)

PREPARATION TIME **10** MINUTES   **35** MINUTES BAKING TIME

A garland of garden-fresh vegetables bakes alongside these succulent game hens, sharing such delightful seasonings as lemon juice, olive oil, rosemary, and garlic. All you need add are steamed green beans.

2 Rock Cornish game hens (1¼ to 1½ lbs. each), split lengthwise
3 tablespoons lemon juice
3 tablespoons olive oil or salad oil
2 teaspoons crumbled dry rosemary
1 clove garlic, minced or pressed
4 shallots, unpeeled
16 to 20 baby carrots, unpeeled
6 to 8 small red thin-skinned potatoes, sliced ¼ inch thick
    Lemon wedges
    Italian parsley

Place game hens, skin sides up, down center of a shallow rimmed 10- by 15-inch baking pan. Mix lemon juice, oil, rosemary, and garlic; pour over game hens. Cut shallots in half lengthwise. Arrange shallots, cut sides down, carrots, and potatoes in a single layer around game hens.

Bake, uncovered, in a 450° oven until meat near thighbone is no longer pink when slashed and vegetables are tender (35 to 40 minutes). Garnish with lemon and parsley. Makes 4 servings.

Per serving: 582 calories, 44 g protein, 31 g carbohydrates, 31 g total fat, 132 mg cholesterol, 160 mg sodium

Braised Cornish Hens in Chianti

PREPARATION TIME **5** MINUTES   **40** MINUTES COOKING TIME

Pancetta, the Italian-style nutmeg-flavored bacon, accents Cornish hens simmered in red wine. Offer a side dish of golden polenta to take advantage of the marvelous sauce.

2 Rock Cornish game hens (1¼ to 1½ lbs. each), split lengthwise
    White pepper
2 tablespoons butter or margarine
1 tablespoon olive oil
2 slices (about 2 oz.) pancetta or bacon, coarsely chopped
1 clove garlic, minced or pressed
½ teaspoon dry marjoram
1 tablespoon tomato paste
1¼ cups Chianti or other dry red wine
1 tablespoon flour
    Chopped parsley

Season game hens with white pepper to taste. In a wide, deep frying pan, melt 1 tablespoon of the butter with oil over medium heat. Add pancetta and cook, stirring often, until lightly browned. With a slotted spoon, remove pancetta, reserving drippings in pan; drain and set aside.

Add game hens to pan and brown over medium-high heat. Spoon off and discard most of the fat. Stir in garlic, marjoram, and tomato paste; add wine. Bring to a boil; reduce heat, cover, and simmer until meat near thighbone is no longer pink when slashed (about 25 minutes). Meanwhile, blend remaining 1 tablespoon butter with flour; set aside.

Lift out game hens, reserving liquid in pan, and transfer to a shallow, ovenproof casserole; sprinkle with pancetta. Keep warm in a 350° oven while preparing sauce. Bring liquid in pan to a boil over high heat, stirring. Blend in butter mixture a little at a time, stirring constantly with a whisk, until sauce is thickened and shiny. Pour over game hens; sprinkle with parsley. Makes 4 servings.

Per serving: 471 calories, 43 g protein, 6 g carbohydrates, 30 g total fat, 151 mg cholesterol, 281 mg sodium

Broiled Tarragon-Turkey Sandwiches

PREPARATION TIME   BROILING TIME

Turn a casual supper into a special occasion with these hot open-faced sandwiches made with mustard-flavored turkey salad. Offer potato chips and crisp raw vegetables to complete the menu.

- ⅓ **cup mayonnaise**
- ¼ **cup Dijon mustard**
- 2 **teaspoons dry tarragon**
- ⅛ **teaspoon ground red pepper (cayenne)**
- 2 **cloves garlic, minced or pressed**
- 2 **cups shredded cooked turkey**
- ½ **cup drained, chopped pickled sweet cherry peppers**
- 3 **English muffins, split**
- 6 **thin slices tomato**
- 6 **thin slices jack cheese (about 2½ inches square *each*)**

Combine mayonnaise, mustard, tarragon, red pepper, and garlic. Add turkey and peppers; mix lightly. Set aside.

Place muffins, cut sides up, on a baking sheet. Broil 4 inches below heat until golden (about 5 minutes). Spread each muffin half with turkey mixture and top with a tomato and a cheese slice.

Return sandwiches to oven and broil until cheese is melted (2 to 3 minutes). Makes 3 servings.

Per serving: 610 calories, 39 g protein, 34 g carbohydrates, 35 g total fat, 111 mg cholesterol, 1791 mg sodium

Swiss Ham & Turkey Melt

Follow directions for Broiled Tarragon-Turkey Sandwiches, but omit 1 clove of the garlic, cherry peppers, English muffins, tomato, and jack cheese.

To turkey mixture add 1 tablespoon chopped **pickled onions.** Substitute split sandwich-size **croissants** for muffins; broil until browned (2½ to 3 minutes). Spread croissants with turkey mixture and top with 6 thin slices cooked **ham** and 6 thin slices **Swiss cheese** (3 to 4 inches square *each*). Broil as directed.

Turkey & Cheese Burgers

PREPARATION TIME   BAKING TIME

As fast and satisfying as any regular cheeseburger, this turkey variation starts with leaner meat. Green chiles, taco sauce, and cumin contribute lively flavor; cottage cheese adds moistness. Serve with all your favorite burger trimmings.

- 1 **pound ground turkey**
- 1 **small can (4 oz.) diced green chiles**
- 1 **cup small curd cottage cheese**
- ¼ **cup fine dry bread crumbs**
- 1 **tablespoon bottled red taco sauce**
- ½ **teaspoon ground cumin**
  Salt and pepper
- 4 **or 5 toasted hamburger buns**

Thoroughly mix turkey, chiles, cottage cheese, bread crumbs, taco sauce, and cumin. Heat a broiler pan with a rack in a 500° oven for 10 minutes.

Meanwhile, divide turkey mixture into 4 or 5 equal portions and shape each into a 3½-inch-wide patty. With a spatula, slide patties onto rack of broiler pan, spacing well apart. Bake, uncovered, until tops are browned and meat in center is no longer pink when cut (about 20 minutes). Let stand for 3 minutes to firm slightly; season with salt and pepper to taste. Place patties, browned sides up, on toasted buns. Makes 4 or 5 servings.

Per serving: 331 calories, 26 g protein, 28 g carbohydrates, 13 g total fat, 67 mg cholesterol, 642 mg sodium

Swiss Turkey & Mushrooms

PREPARATION TIME **20** MINUTES   **15** MINUTES COOKING TIME

If you say *Geschnetzeltes* in the German-speaking part of Switzerland, people may look at you with hungry interest. The word signifies a mouthwatering dish of quickly cooked slivered veal in a brandied cream sauce. Made with turkey breast, the Alpine specialty is equally tempting. Serve with butter-browned potato chunks or fresh egg noodles for a hearty and elegant meal.

1¼ **pounds boneless turkey breast, sliced ½ inch thick**
   Salt and white pepper
   Freshly ground nutmeg
   All-purpose flour
3 **tablespoons butter or margarine**
1 **tablespoon salad oil**
¼ **pound small mushrooms, quartered**
¼ **cup chopped shallots**
¼ **cup dry white wine**
¾ **cup whipping cream**
¼ **cup brandy**
   Chopped parsley

Place turkey slices between sheets of plastic wrap. With a flat-surfaced mallet, pound turkey until about ¼ inch thick. Discard plastic wrap and sprinkle turkey on each side with salt, white pepper, and nutmeg; dust with flour. Cut into thin bite-size strips.

In a wide frying pan, melt 2 tablespoons of the butter with oil over medium-high heat. Cook turkey, about half at a time, until golden brown on all sides. Lift out and set aside.

Add remaining 1 tablespoon butter to pan. Stir in mushrooms and shallots. Cook, stirring often, until mushrooms are lightly browned (about 3 minutes). Add wine and cream. Boil, stirring often, until liquid is reduced by about half. Return turkey and juices to pan. Stir just until heated through, then remove pan from heat.

In a small, long-handled pan, heat brandy until just barely warm. Pour over turkey mixture. Set aflame (*not* beneath an exhaust fan or near flammable items), shaking pan until flames die. Stir turkey mixture over medium-high heat to blend in brandy. Sprinkle with parsley. Makes 4 servings.

Per serving: 430 calories, 36 g protein, 8 g carbohydrates, 28 g total fat, 161 mg cholesterol, 270 mg sodium

Turkey Scaloppine alla Pizzaiola

(Pictured on facing page)

PREPARATION TIME **15** MINUTES   **20** MINUTES COOKING TIME

This zesty entrée goes together almost as quickly as you can say "pizzaiola"—the Neapolitan-style sauce that tops it. If you enjoy veal scaloppine, you'll appreciate this turkey version.

1¼ **pounds boneless turkey breast, sliced ½ inch thick**
   All-purpose flour
1 **egg, beaten with 1 tablespoon water**
2 **tablespoons butter or margarine**
1 **tablespoon olive oil**
¼ **cup grated Parmesan cheese**
   Tomato-Caper Sauce (recipe follows)
   Chopped parsley

Cut turkey into serving-size pieces and place between sheets of plastic wrap. With a flat-surfaced mallet, pound until pieces are about ¼ inch thick. Dust with flour. Dip into egg mixture to coat lightly.

In a wide frying pan, melt 1 tablespoon of the butter with oil over medium-high heat. Add turkey (do not crowd); cook, turning once, until golden brown on both sides. Lift out and arrange on a shallow ovenproof platter, overlapping pieces slightly. Repeat until all turkey is cooked, adding remaining 1 tablespoon butter as needed. Reserve any drippings in pan. Sprinkle turkey with cheese and keep warm in a 325° oven.

Prepare Tomato-Caper Sauce. Spoon over turkey and garnish with parsley. Makes 4 servings.

Tomato-Caper Sauce. Seed and finely chop 3 small **pear-shaped tomatoes.** Heat 1 tablespoon **olive oil** in same pan in which turkey cooked over medium-high heat. Add tomatoes; ½ teaspoon **Italian herb seasoning** or ⅛ teaspoon *each* dry basil, oregano, thyme, and marjoram; 1 clove **garlic,** minced or pressed; 1 tablespoon **tomato paste;** ½ cup **dry white wine;** and 2 teaspoons **capers.** Boil, stirring often, until tomatoes are soft (6 to 8 minutes).

Per serving: 352 calories, 38 g protein, 9 g carbohydrates, 18 g total fat, 176 mg cholesterol, 342 mg sodium

*In Turkey Scaloppine alla Pizzaiola (recipe
on facing page), poultry stands in deliciously for the more
traditional veal. Complement the savory tomato sauce with a side dish of stir-fried zucchini.
For dessert, try Pears, Pepper & Cheese (recipe on page 77).*

Carefree Desserts

Dazzling desserts—frosted layer cakes, cream-filled pastries, fruit pies—don't usually fit into the busy cook's schedule. Leave such works of sugary art to those who have time to indulge in their preparation. But that doesn't mean you'll have to forsake your sweet tooth or the art of dessert-making, even when you're in a hurry. As you shop, learn to look for creamy cheeses and perfectly fresh, beautiful fruits, then practice the sweet skills of dessert spontaneity. You'll create results far more magical than anyone would guess possible in the brief time it takes.

Sherried Cream with Red Grapes

- ⅓ cup sugar
- 2 tablespoons cornstarch
- ⅛ teaspoon salt
- 2 cups milk
- ¼ cup cream sherry or apple juice
- 2 egg yolks, lightly beaten
- 2 tablespoons butter or margarine
- 1 teaspoon vanilla
- 1½ cups seedless red grapes

In a 2-quart pan, stir together sugar, cornstarch, and salt. Gradually blend in milk and sherry. Bring to a boil over medium heat, stirring constantly. Continue boiling and stirring for 1 minute. Remove from heat.

Stir some of the hot sauce into beaten egg yolks in a small bowl; return mixture to pan and cook, stirring constantly, for 30 seconds. Remove from heat and add butter and vanilla, stirring until butter is melted.

Layer spoonfuls of pudding and grapes alternately in 4 stemmed glasses. If made ahead, refrigerate for up to 4 hours. Makes 4 servings.

Per serving: 265 calories, 6 g protein, 33 g carbohydrates, 13 g total fat, 169 mg cholesterol, 193 mg sodium

Sparkling Berries

- 2 cups strawberries, fraises des bois, raspberries, or blackberries, hulled if necessary
  Sparkling muscat wine, chilled

Arrange berries in 4 stemmed glasses. Slowly fill each with wine. Sip wine first and then eat berries with a spoon. Makes 4 servings.

Per serving: 108 calories, .59 g protein, 11 g carbohydrates, .29 g total fat, 0 mg cholesterol, 5 mg sodium

Ginger Cream Sundaes

- ½ cup whipping cream
- 1 tablespoon sugar
- ½ cup preserved ginger in syrup
- 1 pint vanilla ice cream

Beat whipping cream and sugar until cream holds soft peaks. Dice ginger, reserving syrup.

Scoop ice cream into 4 bowls or sundae dishes. Top each serving with a generous dollop of whipped cream, then with ginger and its syrup. Makes 4 servings.

Per serving: 345 calories, 3 g protein, 48 g carbohydrates, 16 g total fat, 63 mg cholesterol, 89 mg sodium

Papaya Sundaes with Lime

- 2 large papayas
- 1 pint vanilla ice cream
  Lime wedges

Cut papayas in half lengthwise; scoop out and discard seeds. Place each papaya half, cut side up, on a salad plate. Fill cavity with ice cream. Serve with lime wedges to squeeze over ice cream and fruit. Makes 4 servings.

Per serving: 194 calories, 3 g protein, 31 g carbohydrates, 7 g total fat, 30 mg cholesterol, 62 mg sodium

Cinnamon Chocolate Sundaes

- 6 ounces Mexican chocolate; or 6 ounces semisweet chocolate and ½ teaspoon ground cinnamon
- ⅔ cup whipping cream
- 2 or 3 small bananas
- 4 or 6 generous scoops vanilla or coffee ice cream

In a 1- to 2-quart pan, combine chocolate and cream. Stir constantly over low heat until chocolate is melted and sauce is smooth; keep warm.

Slice bananas in half crosswise; cut each half lengthwise into 4 pieces. Line each of 4 or 6 small bowls with 4 of the banana spears. Add a scoop of ice cream and top with hot chocolate sauce. Makes 4 or 6 servings.

Per serving: 406 calories, 5 g protein, 44 g carbohydrates, 27 g total fat, 63 mg cholesterol, 74 mg sodium

Berries under Meringue

    Orange-Ginger Sauce (recipe follows)
2 cups strawberries, raspberries, or blackberries, hulled if necessary
2 tablespoons currant-, black raspberry-, or orange-flavored liqueur
3 egg whites
¼ teaspoon cream of tartar
½ cup granulated sugar
1 teaspoon vanilla
1 tablespoon powdered sugar

Prepare Orange-Ginger Sauce; set aside.

Place berries close together in a single layer in center of a 10- to 12-inch ovenproof rimmed platter. Spoon liqueur over berries.

In large bowl of an electric mixer, beat egg whites and cream of tartar at high speed until frothy. Gradually add granulated sugar, beating until stiff peaks form. Beat in vanilla.

Spoon egg whites over berries, mounding so a 1- to 2-inch-wide border of berries remains uncovered. Sift powdered sugar evenly

over meringue. Broil 6 inches below heat until lightly browned (about 3 minutes). Pour sauce around berries on platter. Serve warm. Makes 6 servings.

Orange-Ginger Sauce. In a 1- to 1½-quart pan, stir together ½ cup **sugar** and 1½ tablespoons **cornstarch.** Blend in 1 cup **orange juice** and 3 thin slices (*each* the size of a quarter) **fresh ginger.** Bring to a full boil over high heat, stirring constantly. Remove from heat and discard ginger; stir in 3 tablespoons **lemon juice.** Serve warm (reheat if necessary).

Per serving: 205 calories, 2 g protein, 48 g carbohydrates, .23 g total fat, 0 mg cholesterol, 28 mg sodium

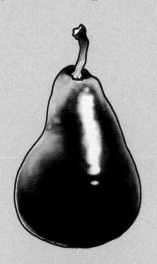

Pears, Pepper & Cheese

(Pictured on page 75)

4 medium-size pears
½ pound buttery blue-veined cheese, such as dolce Gorgonzola or Cambozola (from Bavaria); or double- or triple-cream cheese, such as St. André, l'Explorateur, or Boursault
    Peppermill with black peppercorns or fresh coarse-ground black pepper

Present pears, a chunk of cheese, and peppermill on a plate or board. To eat, slice off a piece of fruit, top with a portion of cheese, and sprinkle with pepper to taste. Makes 4 servings.

Per serving: 297 calories, 9 g protein, 26 g carbohydrates, 19 g total fat, 52 mg cholesterol, 480 mg sodium

Puff Pastry Prune Pies

1 package (10 oz.) frozen puff pastry patty shells
¾ cup (about 8 oz.) marzipan or almond paste
18 moist-pack pitted prunes
⅓ cup sliced almonds
    Vanilla ice cream (optional)

Let patty shells stand in a single layer at room temperature until pliable (about 25 minutes).

Place shells well apart on a large baking sheet. With your fingers, flatten each into a 4-inch-diameter round.

Press 2 tablespoons of the marzipan over top of each pastry. For each pastry, firmly press 3 prunes into marzipan. Sprinkle with almonds. Bake in a 400° oven until golden brown (about 15 minutes). Top with ice cream, if desired, and serve warm. Makes 6 servings.

Per serving: 414 calories, 7 g protein, 46 g carbohydrates, 23 g total fat, 0 mg cholesterol, 227 mg sodium

Meats

For a mouth-watering experience, wrap up stir-fried steak, chiles, and red pepper in a steamy-warm flour tortilla. Top off Fajitas Stir-fry (recipe on facing page) with avocado, sour cream, and a squeeze of fresh lime.

It takes only a few minutes' cooking to transform steaks, chops, sausages, and ground meats to juicy tenderness. All are delicious with only the simplest seasoning. But with a little culinary ingenuity, you can easily elevate plain meats into extraordinary fare. This chapter shows you how to do it—in short order. You'll be amazed at how quickly you can create stylish entrées perfect for any occasion.

Fajitas Stir-fry

(Pictured on facing page)

PREPARATION TIME COOKING TIME

This speedy version of fajitas, a southwestern specialty, starts with stir-frying, rather than grilling, the beef. Papaya Sundaes with Lime (page 76) bring a delicious summer meal to a cool conclusion.

- **8 flour tortillas (8 inches in diameter)**
- **4 tablespoons salad oil**
- **1 pound lean beef steak (about 1 inch thick), such as sirloin or top round, cut across grain into ⅛-inch-thick strips**
- **2 cloves garlic, minced or pressed**
- **1 large onion, thinly sliced into rings**
- **2 or 3 fresh jalapeño chiles, seeded and minced**
- **1 large red bell pepper, seeded and cut into thin strips**
- **2 teaspoons ground cumin**
- **3 tablespoons lime juice**
- **¼ teaspoon salt**
- **1 teaspoon cornstarch**
- **2 medium-size pear-shaped tomatoes, seeded and diced**
  Salt and pepper
- **1 large avocado**
  Lime wedges
  Sour cream

Dampen tortillas lightly with water; wrap in foil and place in a 350° oven until hot and steamy (12 to 15 minutes).

Meanwhile, heat 1 tablespoon of the oil in a wok or wide frying pan over high heat. When oil is hot, add a third of the meat and stir-fry until meat is lightly browned (about 2 minutes). With a slotted spoon, transfer meat to a bowl. Repeat until all meat is browned, adding 2 more tablespoons of the oil.

Add remaining 1 tablespoon oil to pan; then add garlic, onion, chiles, and bell pepper. Stir-fry until onion is tender-crisp (1 to 2 minutes). In a small bowl,

mix cumin, lime juice, the ¼ teaspoon salt, and cornstarch; add to pan along with meat and tomatoes. Cook, stirring, until liquid comes to a boil. Season with salt and pepper to taste. Transfer fajitas to a warm serving dish and keep warm.

Pit, peel, and dice avocado. Spoon meat mixture into warm tortillas and offer avocado, lime, and sour cream to add to taste. Makes 4 servings.

Per serving: 643 calories, 31 g protein, 51 g carbohydrates, 37 g total fat, 68 mg cholesterol, 216 mg sodium

Skewered Beef with Apple & Lettuce

PREPARATION TIME   BROILING TIME

These broiled chunks of tender beef, seasoned with a soy marinade, offer both rich flavor and interesting eating—they're topped with sliced apple, wrapped in lettuce, and eaten out-of-hand.

- **2 pounds boneless beef chuck or top round, fat trimmed**
- **1 cube ginger (1-inch square), peeled and minced**
- **¼ cup soy sauce**
- **2 tablespoons *each* brown sugar and dry white wine**
- **1 tablespoon sesame seeds**
- **1½ teaspoons Oriental sesame oil**
- **1 tablespoon hot chile oil or ½ teaspoon ground red pepper (cayenne)**
- **1 large apple**
  Butter lettuce leaves, washed and crisped

Cut beef into about 1½-inch chunks. Mix ginger, soy sauce, brown sugar, wine, sesame seeds, sesame oil, and chile oil. Stir in beef and let stand for 5 to 10 minutes.

Thread beef onto 4 skewers, dividing equally; reserve marinade. Broil 4 to 6 inches below heat, turning to brown all sides, until beef is browned but still pink in center when cut (about 8 minutes total); brush often with marinade.

Meanwhile, core and slice apple. Line a platter with lettuce leaves. Push beef off skewers onto lettuce. Wrap beef and an apple slice in a lettuce leaf and eat out-of-hand. Makes 4 servings.

Per serving: 358 calories, 35 g protein, 9 g carbohydrates, 19 g total fat, 112 mg cholesterol, 1163 mg sodium

Beef & Chile Stir-fry

PREPARATION TIME **15** MINUTES   **25** MINUTES COOKING TIME

Corn, olives, and chiles tumble with beef in a speedy stir-fry, then top crisp tortilla strips—or, for a leaner version, shredded lettuce.

   Fried Tortilla Strips (recipe follows) or about 2 quarts shredded iceberg lettuce
   Cumin Sauce (recipe follows)
1 **pound lean beef steak (about ¾ inch thick), such as sirloin or top round, cut across grain into ⅛-inch-thick strips**
2 **tablespoons Worcestershire**
3 **cloves garlic, minced or pressed**
4 **tablespoons salad oil**
1 **large onion, thinly sliced**
1 **package (10 oz.) frozen corn kernels, thawed, or about 2 cups corn cut from cob**
1 **can (3 oz.) sliced ripe olives, drained**
1 **large can (7 oz.) diced green chiles, drained**
12 **cherry tomatoes, cut in half**
   Salt
   Fresh cilantro (coriander) sprigs

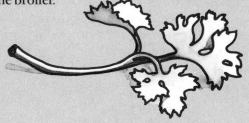

Quick Ways to Cook Steak

There's more than one way to cook steak when time is short. If you stir-fry or sauté atop the range, the steak cooks in minutes. Be sure to heat the pan first, always with a little oil or other fat to protect the finish. Avoid crowding the pan—too much meat can cool off the pan so quickly that the steak exudes precious juices and becomes tough and dry.

Broiling is also a reliably speedy method for cooking steak. Preheat the broiler while you prepare the meat and other ingredients. Then the steak can begin to cook the moment it hits the broiler.

Prepare Fried Tortilla Strips and Cumin Sauce; set aside.

Mix beef strips, Worcestershire, and garlic. Heat 2 tablespoons of the oil in a wok or wide frying pan over high heat. When oil is hot, add half the beef mixture and stir-fry until lightly browned (2 to 3 minutes). With a slotted spoon, transfer beef to a bowl. Repeat until all meat is cooked, adding 1 more tablespoon of the oil.

Add remaining 1 tablespoon oil and onion to pan; stir-fry for 2 minutes. Add corn, olives, and chiles; stir-fry until heated through (2 to 3 minutes). Return meat to pan and add tomatoes and Cumin Sauce; cook, stirring, until juices come to a boil. Season with salt to taste.

Distribute tortilla strips equally on 4 dinner plates. Spoon meat mixture over and garnish with cilantro. Makes 4 servings.

Fried Tortilla Strips. Stack 7 or 8 **corn tortillas** (6 inches in diameter); cut in half. Perpendicular to cut, slice tortillas into ⅛-inch-wide strips. In a medium-size frying pan, pour **salad oil** to a depth of about ½ inch. Place over medium-high heat until oil reaches 375° on a thermometer.

Drop a handful of tortilla strips into oil; cook, stirring, until lightly browned and crisp (about 1 minute). Lift out with a slotted spoon and drain on paper towels. Repeat with remaining tortilla strips until all are cooked. Serve warm or cool. If made ahead, store in a sealed plastic bag until next day. Makes about 2 quarts.

Cumin Sauce. Stir together 2 tablespoons **cornstarch,** 1 teaspoon **cumin seeds,** 1 teaspoon **ground cumin,** ⅛ to ¼ teaspoon **ground red pepper** (cayenne), and 1 cup **regular-strength beef broth.**

Per serving with tortilla strips: 603 calories, 32 g protein, 55 g carbohydrates, 30 g total fat, 68 mg cholesterol, 953 mg sodium

Pepper Beef Stir-fry

PREPARATION TIME **25** MINUTES   **10** MINUTES COOKING TIME

Two kinds of pepper—one adding heat, the other bright color—endow this dish with lively personality. Serve the almost-instant beef creation over fluffy rice.

1 **pound sirloin steak (about 1 inch thick), cut across grain into ⅛-inch-thick strips**
2 **teaspoons cracked pepper**
1 **clove garlic, minced or pressed**
2 **tablespoons Worcestershire**
3 **to 4 tablespoons salad oil**
1 **large onion, thinly sliced**
1 ***each* large red and green bell pepper, seeded and cut into thin strips**
  Salt

Mix beef, pepper, garlic, and Worcestershire; set aside for 15 minutes.

Heat 2 tablespoons of the oil in a wok or wide frying pan over high heat. When oil is hot, add half the meat. Stir-fry until meat is lightly browned (1 to 2 minutes). With a slotted spoon, remove meat from pan and keep warm. Repeat until all meat is cooked, adding more oil if necessary. Add 1 more tablespoon of the oil, onion, and bell peppers to pan; stir-fry just until vegetables are tender-crisp (2 to 3 minutes). Stir in meat and juices. Season with salt to taste. Makes 3 or 4 servings.

Per serving: 506 calories, 20 g protein, 8 g carbohydrates, 44 g total fat, 81 mg cholesterol, 140 mg sodium

Pan-browned Spice Steak

(Pictured on page 83)

PREPARATION TIME **5** MINUTES **40** MINUTES COOKING TIME

A spicy coating of crushed juniper berries, black pepper, and allspice turns simple steak into a connoisseur's choice. Diced sweet potatoes, a mellow accompaniment, hash-brown conveniently in the oven as they bake.

¼ **cup butter or margarine**
4 **medium-size (about 2 lbs.) sweet potatoes or yams, peeled and diced**
1 **tablespoon *each* whole juniper berries, black peppercorns, and whole allspice**
1¼ **to 1½ pounds flank steak or skirt steak, fat trimmed and cut into 4 pieces**
1 **tablespoon salad oil**
2 **tablespoons gin or water**
  Watercress or parsley sprigs
  Pickled onions
  Salt

Place butter in a 10- by 15-inch shallow rimmed baking pan and heat in 450° oven until melted. Add potatoes, stirring to coat with butter. Return to oven and bake, uncovered, until lightly browned and soft when

pressed with a fork (about 30 minutes); turn potatoes several times during baking.

Meanwhile, in a blender or food processor, whirl juniper berries, peppercorns, and allspice until coarsely ground. Press mixture into all sides of each piece of steak.

About 10 minutes before potatoes are done, heat oil in a wide frying pan over medium-high heat. Add steak and cook, turning once, until well browned on both sides and rare in center when cut (3 to 5 minutes total). Lift steaks from pan and keep warm. (To cook steaks more, keep warm in oven with potatoes until meat is done to your liking.)

Add gin to pan, scraping browned bits free. Add potatoes, mixing lightly to coat. Garnish steak and potatoes with watercress and pickled onions. Season with salt to taste. Makes 4 servings.

Per serving: 594 calories, 35 g protein, 40 g carbohydrates, 31 g total fat, 112 mg cholesterol, 257 mg sodium

Broiled Steak with Swiss Mustard Sauce

PREPARATION TIME **5** MINUTES **15** MINUTES BROILING TIME

Thick Porterhouse steak needs only the most subtle sauce, such as this one made from butter, Dijon mustard, and dry vermouth. As you slice the steak, its juices add more flavor.

1 **Porterhouse steak (1½ inches thick)**
3 **tablespoons butter or margarine**
1 **tablespoon Dijon mustard**
2 **tablespoons dry vermouth or dry white wine**
¼ **teaspoon Worcestershire**

Slash through fat edging steak at 2- to 3-inch intervals, cutting just to lean meat. Place steak on a rack in shallow pan. Broil 3 to 4 inches below heat, turning once, until cooked to desired doneness when cut (10 to 14 minutes total for rare to medium-rare).

Meanwhile, in a small pan, melt butter over medium-high heat. Blend in mustard, vermouth, and Worcestershire. Transfer steak to a serving platter; pour sauce around or over meat. Slice steak, swirling cut pieces in sauce. Makes 2 or 3 servings.

Per serving: 442 calories, 28 g protein, 2 g carbohydrates, 35 g total fat, 123 mg cholesterol, 338 mg sodium

Beef with Mushrooms & Madeira Sauce

PREPARATION TIME MINUTES   MINUTES COOKING TIME

This entrée offers elegant eating in both dressed-up and everyday versions. You can prepare it with beef fillet steaks or, for more casual meals, use lean ground beef instead. Accent either version with a salad of avocado and watercress.

- 1½ **pounds lean ground beef or 4 small beef fillet steaks (1 to 1½ inches thick)**
- 1 **tablespoon butter or margarine**
- 1 **tablespoon salad oil**
  French bread
  Additional butter or margarine
- ½ **pound mushrooms, thinly sliced**
- ½ **cup Madeira; or ½ cup regular-strength beef broth and 1½ teaspoons lemon juice**
- ½ **cup whipping cream**

If using ground beef, shape meat into 4 oval patties about 1 inch thick.

In a wide frying pan, melt butter with oil over medium-high heat. Add meat and cook, turning once, until well browned on both sides and cooked to desired doneness (6 to 10 minutes total for rare).

Meanwhile, slice bread diagonally into 4 slices, each about ¾ inch thick. Toast bread, spread with butter, and place a piece on each of 4 dinner plates. Top with meat and keep warm.

Add mushrooms to pan and cook over high heat, stirring, until lightly browned; spoon over meat. Add Madeira and cream to pan and boil, stirring often, until sauce is reduced by about half and slightly thickened; pour sauce over all. Makes 4 servings.

Per serving: 727 calories, 34 g protein, 20 g carbohydrates, 56 g total fat, 180 mg cholesterol, 352 mg sodium

Beef with Mushrooms au Poivre

Follow directions for Beef with Mushrooms & Madeira Sauce, but omit French bread, additional butter, and Madeira.

Coarsely crush 2 teaspoons *each* **whole black peppercorns** and **freeze-dried green peppercorns.** Press into both sides of meat. Cook meat and mushrooms as directed.

Substitute ⅓ cup **brandy** for Madeira. With pan off heat, add brandy; set aflame (*not* beneath an exhaust fan or near flammable items), shaking pan until flames die. Add cream to pan and complete sauce as directed; pour over meat and mushrooms.

Zucchini-crusted Ground Beef Bake

PREPARATION TIME MINUTES   MINUTES BAKING TIME

Let your food processor quickly shred the zucchini and cheese for this extraordinary pizzalike entrée. It's a good summer supper with corn on the cob and iced tea.

- 1½ **pounds medium-size zucchini, shredded (about 4 cups)**
- 2 **eggs**
- 1 **cup (4 oz.) *each* shredded mozzarella and sharp Cheddar cheeses**
- 1 **pound lean ground beef**
- 1 **clove garlic, minced or pressed**
- 1 **medium-size onion, chopped**
- ½ **teaspoon salt**
- 1 **can (8 oz.) tomato sauce**
- 2 **teaspoons dry oregano**
- 1 **green or red bell pepper, seeded and cut into thin strips**
- ¼ **pound mushrooms, sliced**
- ⅓ **cup grated Parmesan cheese**

With your hands, press out any moisture from zucchini. Beat eggs in a large bowl. Lightly mix in zucchini and ½ cup *each* of the mozzarella and Cheddar cheeses. Spread evenly in a lightly greased shallow rimmed 10- by 15-inch baking pan. Bake, uncovered, in a 450° oven for 10 minutes.

Meanwhile, crumble ground beef into a wide frying pan; stir in garlic and onion. Cook over medium-high heat, stirring often, until onion is soft (about 5 minutes); spoon off and discard any excess fat. Stir in salt, tomato sauce, and oregano. Spoon mixture evenly over zucchini crust. Arrange bell pepper and mushrooms evenly over sauce. Sprinkle with remaining mozzarella and Cheddar cheeses; top with Parmesan cheese.

Return to oven and bake until topping is bubbly and lightly browned (about 20 minutes). Cut into squares. Makes 6 servings.

Per serving: 367 calories, 28 g protein, 10 g carbohydrates, 24 g total fat, 175 mg cholesterol, 750 mg sodium

A classic meat-and-potatoes platter rarely
features seasonings as bold and sophisticated as those that
accent Pan-browned Spice Steak (recipe on page 81). With it, serve buttery hash-browned
sweet potatoes, which cook quickly and conveniently in the oven.

Quick Meat Sauce & Green Beans

PREPARATION TIME **7** MINUTES   **35** MINUTES COOKING TIME

Crisp whole green beans stand in for pasta as a bed for this unusual tomato-meat sauce, embellished with anchovies, capers, and ham. Offer hot, buttery garlic bread alongside.

  1 **can (2 oz.) anchovy fillets**
  2 **tablespoons olive oil or salad oil**
  1 **medium-size onion, finely chopped**
  1 **pound lean ground beef or lamb**
  1 **can (14½ oz.) pear-shaped tomatoes**
  ¼ **pound cooked ham, finely chopped**
  1 **tablespoon drained capers**
  ¼ **teaspoon crushed red pepper**
  1 **to 1½ pounds green beans**
  ⅓ **cup grated Parmesan cheese**

Freezing Cooked Meat Mixtures

The fastest dish of all is the one that's already cooked and tucked away in the freezer just waiting for a busy day.

Cooked meat mixtures such as sauces or fillings, stews, and chili are good choices for this kind of advance planning. After cooking, let cool slightly; then seal airtight in a tightly covered freezer container or in a freezer-weight plastic bag. The latter are convenient because for reheating, you can simply immerse them in boiling water, making cleanup a breeze.

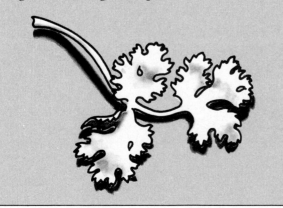

Drain anchovies and mince all but 3 of them; set aside.

Heat oil in a wide frying pan over medium-high heat; add onion and cook, stirring often, until soft (about 5 minutes). Crumble meat into pan; cook, stirring, until meat is well browned (10 to 12 minutes). Spoon off and discard excess fat. Add tomatoes (break up with a spoon) and their liquid, minced anchovies, ham, capers, and pepper. Boil gently, stirring often, until sauce is thickened (about 15 minutes).

Meanwhile, cook beans, uncovered, in a large quantity of boiling salted water until tender-crisp (5 to 8 minutes); drain well.

Arrange beans on a platter. Top with sauce, sprinkle with cheese, and garnish with reserved whole anchovies. Makes 4 servings.

Per serving: 464 calories, 36 g protein, 17 g carbohydrates, 29 g total fat, 98 mg cholesterol, 960 mg sodium

Curry Beef Wrapped in Lettuce

PREPARATION TIME **5** MINUTES   **15** MINUTES COOKING TIME

Inspired by Thai and Chinese cuisines, crisp lettuce leaves enclose hot, curry-seasoned beef and mushrooms in neat, edible bundles. Accompany with rice or thin noodles, either to eat separately or to add to the lettuce wrappers.

  1 **tablespoon salad oil**
  1 **medium-size onion, chopped**
  2 **tablespoons *each* curry powder, tomato paste, and sugar**
  ¾ **pound coarsely ground lean beef**
  2 **ounces mushrooms, chopped**
  2 **tablespoons distilled white vinegar**
     Salt
  1 **medium-size head butter lettuce, washed and crisped**

Heat oil in a wide frying pan over medium-high heat. Add onion and cook, stirring, until edges begin to brown (about 5 minutes). Mix in curry powder, tomato paste, and sugar; stir until mixture is bubbly (about 1 minute). Crumble in meat; add mushrooms and vinegar. Cook, stirring, until most of the liquid has evaporated and meat is no longer pink (about 8 minutes); mixture should still be moist enough to cling together. Season with salt to taste.

Spoon meat mixture into a serving bowl; arrange lettuce leaves in a basket or on a plate. Spoon hot meat into leaves; roll up to eat. Makes 3 or 4 servings.

Per serving: 313 calories, 17 g protein, 13 g carbohydrates, 22 g total fat, 64 mg cholesterol, 128 mg sodium

Borrego Beef & Chorizo Chili

(Pictured on page 86)

PREPARATION TIME COOKING TIME

Named for Borrego Springs, California, its town of origin, this rich, red chili freezes well for a second meal—but it's so good that you probably won't have any leftovers. Thick and meaty, it's more like a stew than a soup.

- 1½ **pounds lean ground beef**
- ½ **pound chorizo sausages, casings removed, sliced ½ inch thick**
- 1 **medium-size onion, sliced**
- 2 **cloves garlic, minced or pressed**
- 3 **to 4 tablespoons chili powder**
- 1 **teaspoon *each* dry oregano and ground cumin**
- 1 **can (about 1 lb.) diced tomatoes in purée**
- 1 **can (1 lb.) kidney beans**
- 1 **can (8 oz.) tomato sauce**
- 4 **to 6 cups shredded iceberg lettuce or corn chips**
  About ⅔ cup *each* shredded jack and sharp Cheddar cheeses

Crumble beef into a 4- to 5-quart pan over medium-high heat; add chorizo. Cook, stirring occasionally, until beef is browned. Spoon off and discard all but about 2 tablespoons of the drippings. Add onion and garlic; cook, stirring, until onion is soft (about 5 minutes). Blend in chili powder, oregano, and cumin; cook, stirring, for 1 more minute.

Stir in tomatoes, kidney beans and juices, and tomato sauce. Bring to a boil; reduce heat, cover, and simmer for 15 minutes, stirring occasionally.

Line individual bowls with lettuce and top with chili. Sprinkle with cheeses. Makes 4 to 6 servings.

Per serving: 609 calories, 38 g protein, 25 g carbohydrates, 40 g total fat, 119 mg cholesterol, 1121 mg sodium

To Microwave: Crumble beef into a 3- to 4-quart microwave-safe casserole; add chorizo. Microwave, uncovered, on **HIGH (100%)** for 8 to 10 minutes, stirring 2 or 3 times, until beef is no longer pink. Spoon off and discard most of the drippings. Stir in onion, garlic, chili powder, oregano, and cumin. Microwave, uncovered, on **HIGH (100%)** for 3 to 5 minutes, stirring once or twice, until onion is soft.

Stir in tomatoes, kidney beans and their juices, and tomato sauce. Microwave, covered, on **HIGH (100%)** for 12 to 15 minutes or until chili is bubbly all over. Let stand, covered, for 3 to 5 minutes. Serve as directed.

Sausage & Salsa Rolls

PREPARATION TIME   COOKING TIME

Sandwiches, like tacos, benefit from a lively fresh salsa. Here, sautéed slices of Polish sausage, topped with coarse mustard, rest on a crusty roll that's been spread with a cilantro and chile salsa. Just add a glass of cool dry white or rosé wine.

- **Cilantro Salsa (recipe follows)**
- 2 **Polish or linguisa sausages (4 to 5 oz. *each*)**
- 2 **round crusty rolls (4 to 5 inches in diameter), split horizontally**
  Coarsely ground prepared mustard
  Mayonnaise (optional)

Prepare Cilantro Salsa and set aside. If made ahead, cover and refrigerate until next day.

Cut sausages into ⅜-inch-thick diagonal slices. Lay slices in a wide frying pan and cook over medium heat, turning once, until lightly browned on both sides.

Meanwhile, broil rolls, cut sides up, about 4 inches below heat until toasted.

Spoon about 2 tablespoons of the salsa onto bottom half of each roll. Place sausage slices on top and add a dollop of mustard. If desired, spread roll tops with mayonnaise. Offer remaining salsa to add to taste. Serve open-faced or closed, with a knife and fork. Makes 2 servings.

Cilantro Salsa. In a blender or food processor, combine ¼ cup *each* **lime juice** and **salad oil;** 1 cup packed **fresh cilantro (coriander) leaves;** 1 small hot **fresh** or pickled **chile,** such as serrano or jalapeño, stemmed and seeded; ¼ cup chopped **onion;** and 1 clove **garlic,** minced or pressed. Whirl mixture until puréed. Season with **salt** to taste. Makes about 1 cup.

Per serving: 731 calories, 27 g protein, 42 g carbohydrates, 50 g total fat, 101 mg cholesterol, 1650 mg sodium

Cool off its spicy fire by spooning Borrego
Beef & Chorizo Chili (recipe on page 85) over shredded lettuce
or, for a change, crisp tortilla chips. Offer cold, light Mexican beer
alongside this simple, yet sensational, entrée.

Joe's Sausage & Greens with Eggs

PREPARATION TIME **20** MINUTES **15** MINUTES COOKING TIME

Any San Franciscan knows that Joe's Special means a dish made with eggs, spinach, and ground beef. This version substitutes red Swiss chard and Italian sausage, but still makes a delicious partner for crusty San Francisco sourdough bread.

> 2 **tablespoons salad oil**
> 1 **pound mild or hot Italian sausages, casings removed**
> 2 **large onions, finely chopped**
> 2 **cloves garlic, minced or pressed**
> ½ **pound mushrooms, thinly sliced**
> ¼ **teaspoon** *each* **ground nutmeg, pepper, and dry oregano**
> 1 **pound red Swiss chard, cut into thin shreds (about 8 cups)**
> 8 **eggs**
> **Salt**
> 1 **cup (4 oz.) shredded jack cheese**

Heat oil in a wok or wide frying pan over high heat. Crumble sausages into pan. Stir-fry until meat is well browned. Add onions, garlic, mushrooms, nutmeg, pepper, and oregano; cook, stirring often, until onion is limp and all the liquid has evaporated. Stir in chard, a portion at a time, starting with stems, and cook until chard is just wilted (3 to 4 minutes).

Beat eggs in a bowl. Add to chard mixture and stir over low heat just until eggs are softly set. Season with salt to taste. Sprinkle with cheese. Makes 4 to 6 servings.

Per serving: 522 calories, 26 g protein, 10 g carbohydrates, 42 g total fat, 439 mg cholesterol, 910 mg sodium

To Microwave: Omit salad oil. Crumble sausages into a 4-quart microwave-safe casserole; add onions, garlic, mushrooms, nutmeg, pepper, and oregano. Microwave on **HIGH (100%)** for 10 to 12 minutes, stirring once or twice, until sausage is no longer pink; spoon off and discard most of the liquid.

Stir in chard all at once; cover and let stand. Beat eggs, using only 6. Stir beaten eggs into casserole. Microwave on **HIGH (100%)** for 10 to 12 minutes, stirring 2 or 3 times to bring cooked portion of eggs to inside of dish, until eggs are softly set. Add salt and cheese as directed.

Upside-down Pizza

PREPARATION TIME **10** MINUTES   **35** MINUTES COOKING TIME

For all the pleasures of home-baked pizza but with much less time and effort, try this hearty casserole version topped with a puffy golden-brown crust. Serve with a crisp, leafy salad and beer or red wine.

> 1 **pound mild or hot Italian sausages, casings removed**
> 1 **medium-size onion, chopped**
> 1 **jar (15½ oz.) spaghetti sauce**
> ½ **pound mushrooms, sliced**
> 1 **can (2¼ oz.) sliced ripe olives, drained**
> 1 **package (6 oz.) sliced mozzarella cheese**
> 2 **eggs**
> 1 **cup** *each* **all-purpose flour and milk**
> 1 **tablespoon salad oil**
> ¼ **teaspoon salt**
> ¼ **cup grated Parmesan cheese**

Crumble sausages into a wide frying pan over medium-high heat. Add onion and cook, stirring often, until onion is soft and sausages are well browned (8 to 10 minutes). Spoon off and discard fat, if necessary. Stir in spaghetti sauce, mushrooms, and olives. Cook until bubbly; then spread in an ungreased 9- by 13-inch baking dish or pan. Arrange mozzarella over top.

In a blender or food processor, combine eggs, flour, milk, oil, and salt; whirl until smooth. Pour evenly over mozzarella and sprinkle with Parmesan cheese.

Bake, uncovered, in a 425° oven until crust is puffy and golden brown (about 20 minutes). Cut into squares to serve. Makes 4 to 6 servings.

Per serving: 534 calories, 26 g protein, 34 g carbohydrates, 33 g total fat, 165 mg cholesterol, 1256 mg sodium

Cheese-crusted Chili Beef

Follow directions for Upside-down Pizza, but omit sausages, onion, spaghetti sauce, mushrooms, olives, mozzarella, and Parmesan cheese.

Crumble 1 pound **lean ground beef** into pan and brown with 1 **red onion,** chopped, and 1 tablespoon **chili powder.** Stir in 1 large can (15 oz.) **tomato sauce** and 1 large can (7 oz.) **diced green chiles.** Instead of mozzarella, top meat mixture with 1 package (6 oz.) **sliced jack cheese.** After adding batter topping, sprinkle with ½ cup shredded **Cheddar cheese.** Bake as directed.

Oriental Pocket Bread Sandwiches

PREPARATION TIME **15** MINUTES   **10** MINUTES COOKING TIME

Stir-fry strips of pork or beef to make the marvelously seasoned Oriental filling for these pocket bread sandwiches. As an accompaniment, offer mugs of steaming puréed vegetable soup.

>   3   pocket bread rounds, cut in half
>   1   tablespoon cornstarch
>   2   tablespoons *each* soy sauce and dry sherry
>   1   teaspoon sugar
>   ⅓   cup water
>   2   tablespoons salad oil
>   ¾   pound boneless pork or beef, cut into thin 1- by 3-inch strips
>   2   cloves garlic, minced or pressed
>   2   teaspoons minced fresh ginger or 1 teaspoon ground ginger
>   ¼   teaspoon pepper
>   ½   pound bean sprouts
>   ⅓   cup thinly sliced green onions (including tops)

Wrap pocket bread in foil; heat in a 350° oven while preparing filling.

Stir together cornstarch, soy sauce, sherry, sugar, and water; set aside.

Heat oil in a wok or wide frying pan over high heat. When oil is hot, add pork, garlic, ginger, and pepper; stir-fry until meat is lightly browned (3 to 4 minutes). Add cornstarch mixture and cook, stirring constantly, until sauce thickens and boils. Gently mix in bean sprouts and onions.

Spoon filling into a warm serving bowl. Spoon into warm pocket bread halves. Makes 3 servings (2 sandwiches each).

Per serving: 622 calories, 30 g protein, 48 g carbohydrates, 34 g total fat, 79 mg cholesterol, 1119 mg sodium

To Microwave: Place pocket bread halves in a plastic bag; set aside.

Reduce water to ¼ cup and combine with cornstarch, soy sauce, sherry, and sugar in a 1- to 2-cup glass measure; set aside.

Omit salad oil. Combine pork, garlic, ginger, and pepper in a 3-quart microwave-safe casserole. Microwave, covered, on **HIGH (100%)** for 4 to 5 minutes, stirring once or twice, until meat is no longer pink.

Spoon off liquid from pork and add to cornstarch mixture. Microwave liquid mixture, uncovered, on **HIGH (100%)** for 2 to 2½ minutes or until bubbly, thickened, and clear. Add sauce to pork. Stir in bean sprouts and onions. Microwave, uncovered, on **HIGH (100%)** for 2 to 3 minutes or until heated through. Cover and set aside.

Microwave pocket bread on **HIGH (100%)** for 30 to 45 seconds or until heated through. Serve as directed.

Sautéed Pork with Red Peppers

(Pictured on page 91)

PREPARATION TIME **15** MINUTES   **30** MINUTES COOKING TIME

A burst of fresh lemon juice and a light, garlicky sauce give this tender boneless pork a zesty accolade. Add more color and flavor to the menu with a side dish of butter-steamed zucchini.

>   2   pounds boneless center-cut pork loin, fat trimmed and cut into ½-inch-thick slices
>   4   cloves garlic, minced or pressed
>   Pepper
>   2   tablespoons butter or margarine
>   4   medium-size red bell peppers (about 1½ lbs. *total*), seeded and cut into thin strips
>   2   tablespoons salad oil
>   ¾   cup *each* dry white wine and regular-strength chicken broth
>   Lemon wedges
>   Italian parsley

Sprinkle pork with garlic and season with pepper to taste. Set aside.

In a wide frying pan, melt butter over medium-high heat. Add bell pepper strips and cook, stirring often, until limp (about 10 minutes). Transfer to a platter and keep warm.

Add 1 tablespoon of the oil to pan; increase heat to high. Add pork; do not crowd. Cook, turning once, until browned on both sides (about 3 minutes total). Lift out pork and arrange on platter with peppers, scraping browned bits free. Repeat until all pork is cooked, adding remaining oil as needed. Reserve drippings in pan.

Add wine and broth to pan. Boil, stirring often, until sauce is reduced to ½ cup (6 to 8 minutes). Pour over

meat and peppers. Garnish with lemon and parsley.
Makes 4 servings.

*Per serving: 450 calories, 42 g protein, 10 g carbohydrates,
26 g total fat, 129 mg cholesterol, 373 mg sodium*

Pork Medallions with Prunes

PREPARATION TIME   COOKING TIME

Present each plump, prune-garnished pork medallion
with sprigs of vivid watercress and offer steamed rice
alongside.

- **1 pound pork tenderloin, surface fat trimmed
  and cut across grain into 1-inch-thick slices**
- **¾ cup Madeira**
- **½ cup regular-strength beef broth**
- **1 tablespoon red wine vinegar**
- **2 teaspoons cornstarch**
- **3 whole cloves**
- **2 tablespoons butter or margarine**
- **12 pitted prunes**
- **⅓ cup chopped shallots
  Watercress sprigs
  Salt**

Place meat slices between sheets of plastic wrap. With
a flat-surfaced mallet, gently pound meat until slices
are about ⅜ inch thick.

Stir together Madeira, broth, vinegar, cornstarch,
and cloves; set aside.

In a wide frying pan, melt butter over medium-high
heat. Add pork (do not crowd); cook, turning once,
until lightly browned on both sides and no longer
pink in center when cut (4 to 6 minutes total). Transfer
meat to a plate and keep warm. Repeat until all pork is
cooked. When pan is almost empty, add prunes, turning in drippings to warm. With a slotted spoon, lift
out prunes and remaining pork, reserving drippings
in pan.

Add shallots to pan and cook, stirring, until limp.
Add Madeira mixture and any juices that have accumulated from pork. Cook, stirring, until sauce comes to
a boil.

Arrange pork and prunes on 3 or 4 warm dinner
plates; spoon sauce over meat and fruit. Garnish with
watercress and season with salt to taste. Makes 3 or 4
servings.

*Per serving: 271 calories, 25 g protein, 23 g carbohydrates,
9 g total fat, 89 mg cholesterol, 235 mg sodium*

Pork Tenderloin with Stilton, Port & Jalapeños

PREPARATION TIME   COOKING TIME

Stilton cheese and port wine are classic partners.
Here, slivered jalapeño chiles add a note of impu-
dence to their elegance as the three bold ingredients
combine to accent roast pork tenderloin. Accompany
with baked sweet potatoes or the hash-browned sweet
potatoes in Pan-browned Spice Steak (see page 81).

- **1 tablespoon salad oil**
- **1½ pounds pork tenderloin, surface fat
  trimmed**
- **1 cup port**
- **½ cup regular-strength chicken broth**
- **½ cup whipping cream**
- **¼ pound Stilton cheese, crumbled**
- **1 or 2 fresh jalapeño chiles, halved
  lengthwise, seeded, and cut into slivers**

Heat oil in a wide frying pan over medium-high heat.
Add pork and brown well on all sides. Transfer to a 9-
or 10-inch square baking pan. Bake, uncovered, in a
400° oven until a meat thermometer inserted in thickest part registers 160° (about 15 minutes).

Meanwhile, discard fat in frying pan and add port
and broth. Boil over high heat until reduced to ¾ cup
(about 3 minutes). Stir in cream and continue to boil
until large shiny bubbles form (about 5 minutes). Add
cheese and chiles; stir until cheese is melted. Remove
from heat and keep warm.

Slice meat across grain; fan slices on 4 warm dinner
plates. Spoon sauce over meat. Makes 4 servings.

*Per serving: 458 calories, 46 g protein, 8 g carbohydrates,
26 g total fat, 179 mg cholesterol, 625 mg sodium*

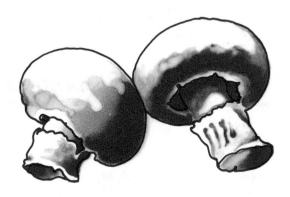

Grilled Veal Chops & Vegetables

PREPARATION TIME **5** MINUTES   **10** MINUTES COOKING TIME

Looking like miniature T-bone steaks, veal loin chops grill to succulent perfection. Here, they share the pan—and a lemony baste—with Japanese eggplant and green onions. To complete an effortless dinner for two, add small baked potatoes.

- 1 **tablespoon lemon juice**
- 2 **tablespoons olive oil or salad oil**
- ¼ **teaspoon dry marjoram**
- 1 **clove garlic, minced or pressed**
- 1 **small Japanese-type eggplant (about 6 inches long), unpeeled**
- 2 **veal loin chops, about 1 inch thick (about 1 lb. *total*)**
- 4 **green onions (including tops) or baby leeks, ends trimmed**
  Lemon zest
  Salt and freshly ground pepper

Blend lemon juice, olive oil, marjoram, and garlic. Cut eggplant in half lengthwise. Brush veal chops, eggplant, and onions generously with oil mixture.

Place a ridged cooktop grill pan over medium-high heat and preheat until a drop of water dances on surface. Place chops in center of pan; add eggplant, cut sides down, and onions around chops. Cook, turning each ingredient once, until onions are tender-crisp (4 to 5 minutes total), chops are well browned on both sides and barely pink inside when cut near bone (6 to 8 minutes total), and eggplant is tender (about 8 minutes total).

Arrange veal and vegetables on warm dinner plates. Sprinkle each serving with lemon zest and season with salt and pepper to taste. Makes 2 servings.

Per serving: 456 calories, 37 g protein, 5 g carbohydrates, 32 g total fat, 136 mg cholesterol, 92 mg sodium

Veal with Wild Mushrooms

PREPARATION TIME **15** MINUTES   **20** MINUTES COOKING TIME

Why is everyone going wild over wild mushrooms? Here's your chance to find out—or to savor them again. This recipe brings out the subtle flavors of these mushrooms, now appearing in gourmet produce markets in ever greater variety. Cut larger ones in half or into quarters before cooking. (You can substitute standard button mushrooms, sliced or quartered, if you prefer.)

- 1¼ **pounds boneless veal leg, sliced ½ inch thick**
  All-purpose flour
- 3 **tablespoons butter or margarine**
  About 2 tablespoons salad oil
- 1 **small clove garlic, minced or pressed**
- ¼ **pound wild mushrooms (such as shiitake, angel trumpets, chanterelles, oyster mushrooms, or morels), trimmed, rinsed, and patted dry**
- ¼ **teaspoon *each* salt and dry tarragon**
- ⅛ **teaspoon white pepper**
- 1 **tablespoon lemon juice**
- ¼ **cup Calvados or brandy**
- ½ **cup whipping cream**
- 2 **to 3 cups hot cooked rice**

Trim and discard any tough membrane from meat; cut into serving-size pieces. Place meat between sheets of plastic wrap. With a flat-surfaced mallet, gently pound meat until slices are about ⅛ inch thick. Dust each piece lightly with flour.

In a wide frying pan, melt 2 tablespoons of the butter with 1 tablespoon of the oil over medium-high heat. Add veal; do not crowd. Cook, turning once, until well browned on both sides (4 to 5 minutes total). Arrange slices, overlapping slightly, around edge of an ovenproof platter. Repeat until all veal is cooked, adding up to 1 more tablespoon oil as needed. Keep veal warm in a 200° oven. Remove pan with drippings from heat.

Add remaining 1 tablespoon butter to pan. Stir in garlic and mushrooms and cook over medium-high heat, stirring gently, until mushrooms are lightly browned and most of the liquid has evaporated (2 to 3 minutes). Sprinkle with salt, tarragon, white pepper, and lemon juice. Add Calvados and set aflame (*not* beneath an exhaust fan or near flammable items), shaking pan until flames die. Add cream; boil, stirring often, until sauce is slightly thickened (about 2 minutes).

Mound rice in center of platter; spoon mushroom sauce over veal. Makes 4 servings.

Per serving: 643 calories, 33 g protein, 44 g carbohydrates, 36 g total fat, 157 mg cholesterol, 333 mg sodium

Stir-fried ribbons of bell peppers, a light
wine sauce, and the robust pungency of garlic distinguish
Sautéed Pork with Red Peppers (recipe on page 88). Crusty French bread
contributes quiet balance to this festive entrée.

Veal with Olives & Dried Tomatoes

(Pictured on front cover)

PREPARATION TIME **20** MINUTES   **15** MINUTES COOKING TIME

Vivid in both color and taste, a blend of dried tomatoes and salty, oil-cured olives crowns this tender veal scaloppine. Serve the sophisticated sauté with hot, buttered spinach fettucine and accompany with crisp bread sticks and a light red wine.

1¼	**pounds boneless veal leg, cut across grain into 8 equal slices**
	Olives & Dried Tomatoes (recipe follows)
¾	**cup fine dry bread crumbs**
1	**tablespoon chopped parsley**
¾	**teaspoon pepper**
1	**egg**
½	**cup milk**
2	**tablespoons butter or margarine**
	Salt
	Lemon wedges

Trim and discard any tough membrane from meat. Place veal between sheets of plastic wrap. With a flat-surfaced mallet, gently pound meat until slices are ⅛ inch thick. Prepare Olives & Dried Tomatoes and set aside.

Mix bread crumbs, parsley, and pepper in a shallow pan. In another shallow pan, beat egg with milk. Dip veal in egg mixture to coat; drain briefly. Then coat with crumbs. Place meat in a single layer on wax paper.

Drain and reserve oil from olive mixture. Heat half the oil with 1 tablespoon of the butter in a wide frying pan over medium-high heat. Add veal; do not crowd. Cook, turning once, until richly browned on both

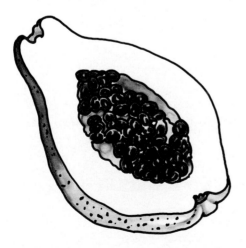

sides (4 to 5 minutes total). Arrange veal on a warm platter, overlapping slices slightly, and keep warm. Repeat until all veal is cooked, adding remaining oil and remaining 1 tablespoon butter as needed. If made ahead, keep veal warm in a 200° oven for up to 20 minutes.

Top veal with olive mixture. Season with salt to taste and garnish with lemon. Makes 4 servings.

Olives & Dried Tomatoes. In a medium-size frying pan, combine 2 tablespoons *each* **salad oil** and **olive oil**, ¼ cup chopped **dried tomatoes packed in oil**, and ¼ cup chopped **oil-cured black ripe olives** over low heat. Stir until oil takes on flavors of olives and tomatoes (8 to 10 minutes). Use warm or at room temperature.

Per serving: 568 calories, 33 g protein, 17 g carbohydrates, 40 g total fat, 190 mg cholesterol, 608 mg sodium

Broiled Lamb Chops with Papaya Chutney

(Pictured on page 94)

PREPARATION TIME **15** MINUTES   **20** MINUTES COOKING TIME

Lamb and fruit create a marriage of flavors extolled in many cuisines. Let the season guide your choice of fruit for our quick chutney: nectarines or peaches in summer, juicy papaya in winter.

	Seasoned Yogurt (recipe follows)
8	**to 10 single rib lamb chops (1½ to 2 lbs. *total*), fat trimmed**
	Salt and pepper
¼	**cup *each* sugar and cider vinegar**
1	**small onion, minced**
½	**cup raisins**
1	**teaspoon *each* ground cinnamon and ground ginger**
1	**large papaya or 3 medium-size nectarines or peaches (about 1 lb.), peeled, seeded or pitted, and sliced ¼ inch thick**
1	**large cucumber, seeded and cut into strips (optional)**

Prepare Seasoned Yogurt; set aside.

Broil lamb chops about 4 inches below heat, turning once, until well browned on both sides but still pink inside when cut (6 to 8 minutes total). Season with salt and pepper to taste.

Meanwhile, in a wide frying pan, combine sugar, vinegar, onion, raisins, cinnamon, and ginger. Cook over medium-high heat, stirring often, until onion is soft and raisins are plump (about 5 minutes). Add papaya and stir gently until heated through (about 3 minutes). Spoon papaya mixture over lamb chops or serve in a separate bowl. Offer Seasoned Yogurt and, if desired, cucumber strips alongside. Makes 4 servings.

Seasoned Yogurt. Combine 2 cups **plain yogurt,** ¼ teaspoon **chili powder,** ½ teaspoon **ground cumin,** 1 teaspoon **sugar,** and 1 tablespoon **mustard seeds;** stir until well blended.

Per serving of lamb and chutney: 320 calories, 24 g protein, 37 g carbohydrates, 9 g total fat, 85 mg cholesterol, 62 mg sodium

Per tablespoon of Seasoned Yogurt: 11 calories, .82 g protein, 1 g carbohydrate, .31 g total fat, .85 mg cholesterol, 10 mg sodium

Olive-crusted Lamb Chops

PREPARATION TIME   COOKING TIME

A robust relish from the south of France, *tapenade* brings together black olives, mustard, anchovies, and herbs. It enhances many meats—such as these thick lamb chops, which bake at high temperature as if they were single-portion roasts. Alongside, serve crisp, pan-browned potatoes and a salad of watercress.

> 4 **lamb rib chops, about 2 inches thick (about 2 lbs. *total*)**
> **Tapenade (recipe follows)**

With a sharp knife, cut through fat on edges of chops at 1-inch intervals. Lay chops, fat sides up, on edge (they can lean against one another for support) in a shallow rimmed 10- by 15-inch baking pan. Broil 3 inches below heat until fat is lightly browned (8 to 10 minutes). Remove from oven.

Meanwhile, prepare Tapenade.

Drain and discard any fat from pan. Lay chops flat, well apart; firmly pat 1 tablespoon of the relish onto meaty part of each chop. Turn chops over and coat with 1 more tablespoon of the relish. Bake in a 500° oven until rare in center when cut (about 10 minutes) or until done to your liking. Serve chops with remaining relish. Makes 2 or 4 servings.

Tapenade. Measure ½ cup **oil-cured black ripe olives;** cut meat from pits. (Or use ½ cup drained canned and pitted black ripe olives.) In a food processor or blender, combine olives, ¼ cup drained **capers,** 2 teaspoons **Dijon mustard,** 5 drained canned

anchovy fillets, ¼ teaspoon *each* **cracked bay leaves** and **dry thyme,** and 1 large clove **garlic,** minced or pressed. Whirl until mixture is finely chopped but not puréed.

Per serving: 251 calories, 25 g protein, 2 g carbohydrates, 16 g total fat, 88 mg cholesterol, 951 mg sodium

Baked Lamb Meatballs with Pine Nuts

PREPARATION TIME   COOKING TIME

These lamb meatballs bake quickly in a hot oven and then are smothered in a sweet-sour red onion sauce. As a perfect dinner partner, serve buttered fresh pasta liberally sprinkled with Parmesan cheese.

> 1 **egg**
> ½ **teaspoon *each* salt and ground cinnamon**
> 1 **clove garlic, minced or pressed**
> 2 **tablespoons *each* fine dry bread crumbs and catsup**
> 1 **tablespoon red wine vinegar**
> ¼ **cup pine nuts or slivered almonds**
> 1½ **pounds lean ground lamb**
> 1 **tablespoon olive oil**
> 1 **small red onion, thinly sliced**
> ½ **cup Marsala or cream sherry**
> 2 **teaspoons lemon juice**
> **Chopped parsley**

Beat egg until blended; mix in salt, cinnamon, garlic, bread crumbs, catsup, and vinegar. Add pine nuts and lamb; mix lightly. Shape mixture into 1½-inch meatballs. Set slightly apart in a shallow rimmed baking pan. Bake in a 500° oven until well browned (10 to 12 minutes).

Meanwhile, heat oil in a medium-size frying pan over medium heat. Add onion and cook, stirring often, until soft and lightly browned (6 to 8 minutes). Remove pan from heat and set aside.

With a slotted spoon, transfer meatballs to a warm serving dish and keep warm. Pour off and discard fat from baking pan. Pour a little of the wine into baking pan, scraping browned bits free; add to onion mixture along with remaining wine and lemon juice. Boil over high heat, stirring, until liquid is reduced by about half. Pour over meatballs and sprinkle with parsley. Makes 4 servings.

Per serving: 537 calories, 30 g protein, 10 g carbohydrates, 42 g total fat, 186 mg cholesterol, 468 mg sodium

Contrasting flavors combine deliciously in
Broiled Lamb Chops with Papaya Chutney (recipe on page 92),
presented here over Almond Pilaf with Sherry (recipe on page 52). In summer,
you can prepare the chutney with nectarines or peaches instead of papaya.

Index